Keeping Your Job

While Your Bosses Are

Losing Theirs

Marylou Hughes

WN
WILLIAM
· NEIL ·
Publishing

Binghamton, New York

5-19-99

All examples are based on actual occurrences; however, names have been changed to protect the anonymity of individuals.

Printed in the United States of America.

Library of Congress Catalog Number: 97-076252

ISBN 0-9642806-1-2

1998

Keeping Your Job

For
Dr. Evans Harrell
and
Dr. Janice Harrell

CONTENTS

PREFACE

With three personally and professionally wrenching exceptions, I have held jobs that allowed me to work with people and bosses whom I could easily praise and with whom I truly enjoyed working. I handled my dissatisfaction in the first two of these exceptions by leaving; by the third, I had learned some valuable lessons and decided that there was a better way of dealing with the situation than heading out the door with another job lined up. I had by then reviewed my behavior and my coworkers' actions in the past two situations and recognized how I compounded my troubles. I started testing techniques for taking charge of disturbing employment problems.

I also learned about new management and difficult adjustments through professional contacts with psychotherapy clients, consultation with health professionals, and teaching students in management courses. They, like my coworkers and I, made mistakes that added to their own misery.

The approaches I used for dealing with new management my third time around were effective and, just as important, they helped me feel as though I was in control and doing something about the problem. And I guess I was—I still do some work for that organization.

This book is focused totally on survival, i.e., keeping the job. Nevertheless, the material is helpful to anyone newly employed, starting a different job, getting a promotion, or wanting to know what to do to impress the boss.

Some might argue that these approaches do not actually give the employees control over their future. I contend, however that they do, in fact, give the workers sole control over their own destiny. Jobholders feel the power of their decisions when they subscribe to the approaches suggested in this book. However, it is a matter of choice. The safe and peaceful way I am advocating may not be the way everybody wants to go. Those with power and influence may be able to risk direct challenges, recruit and use coalitions, or decide to pursue legal avenues to exercise their rights. But I believe there is an easier way, one that leads to a positive result, and that is what this book is about: How to keep your job while your bosses are losing theirs.

About the Author

Dr. Marylou Hughes is a psychotherapist in private practice in Ft. Pierce, Florida, and a consultant to health care agencies. She provides professional help to many who struggle to adjust to changed working conditions and as an Employment Assistance Counselor is in touch with work problems on an almost daily basis. She has personally experienced the trauma of new management and used many of the approaches detailed in this book.

CHAPTER 1

Understanding Change

Change in the workplace is not a matter of choice, but a fact of life. Change has always been part of the work situation and is more so today because companies have to keep up with rapidly changing times. Companies that are competitive and prosper are those that are responsive to these changes and employ a flexible workforce.

It is unlikely anybody escapes new management. Large corporations have, as a matter of practice, moved their managers around to test their ability, reward them for their service, and keep them interested. But corporations themselves are in a state of flux. In the first four years of the 90s there was an average of 3,500 mergers and acquisitions per year (Department of Commerce, 1996). This, of course, has resulted in a lot of new management. But new management can mean anything from a takeover by another company to promotions from inside or hires from the outside. The Chief Executive Officer (CEO) experiences new management when there is a new chairman of the board. "New management" implies there is a different person in charge, but such is not always the case. Personnel may remain the same, but policies and procedures can change, as happens when a company reinvents itself, governmental policies and politics change, small businesses are bought out by larger corporations, or the situation requires different approaches to achieve goals or maintain economic health.

Change is not instigated with the employee's well-being in mind. Change is effected to keep a company viable and productive, usually in response to outside pressures, or because of business and financial benefits. As a matter of fact, reports indicate the American worker is losing ground in salary and security (Crutsinger, 1996). This is because managers implement changes which they envision will keep their companies prosperous. They hire temporary help, contract with specialists outside the company, do away with top heavy management, decentralize, and expect employees to do more with less. Change is not good for everyone, but it is inevitable. At any stage in one's work life, starting with one's first job, there will be and continue to be change. This is part and parcel of the process of adjusting to a job. Changes occur often and result in new people, policies, procedures, and products. The sooner the new or seasoned employee adjusts to these changes, the sooner that employee becomes an asset to the company.

CHANGE IS THE GIVEN

In the past the "average 65-year-old American man held 10.7 jobs in his lifetime, and the average 65-year-old American woman held 12.2" (Boyd, 1996: D2). Present day change moves at a faster pace. Entrepreneurial companies see stagnation as more dangerous than making a mistake. It is better to act than be left behind. Companies get rid of unwanted properties, sell off the poor producers, and look for more profitable ventures. Since this is the mode of present day business, employees can expect to work with many different people, bosses, and management styles. Patience is out. Productivity is in. The workplace is fast-paced, competitive, and demanding. It supports employees who work harder, respond positively to pressure, work well with others, and can live with uncertainty. Employees cannot count on the corporation furnishing them permanent security. Tom Peters (1992) states that only fickle decentralized companies are able to compete in a fickle decentralized economy. He sees evidence of business success in companies that employ teams to work on projects, with the teams changing in function and size as needed, depending on the project. Team members are cross-trained and autonomous, giving each other support and relying on each other's skill.

New managers are different from past managers. Their major interest is in "reducing costs by becoming leaner, changing the business mix to gain greater focus, discontinuing or contracting out activities unrelated to their core competence, and more flexibly moving into and out of businesses" (Kanter, 1989: 57). The employees comply or they look elsewhere.

Will this trend change? Possibly, but not in the near future. Right now competition is global and companies are governed by outside rules and regulations and the demands of consumers, activists, and stockholders. "[R]estructuring is a continuing process, almost a corporate fitness regimen" (Kanter, 1989: 58).

Restructuring and change is not specific to major corporations. It happens all over and in all areas of production, whether the final product is service, goods, or educated people. Health care providers, manufacturers, financial institutions, government service agencies, large and small businesses, transportation providers, and educational institutions experience change and must be responsive if they are to stay in business and make a profit. The workers' choice is not whether to accept change, but how to accommodate change. Energy must be invested in adapting to, rather than fighting, change.

EMOTIONAL REACTIONS

There is no question that people react emotionally to change. The question is how best to deal with the emotional reactions. Any kind of change, sad or happy, causes stress. Changes that affect our economical well-being are particularly stressful (Ornstein and Sobel, 1987). Change in the workplace is aggravated by feelings of being ignored, fear of what may happen, frustration with unwanted alterations, and the contagious anxiety of coworkers. Anger results as the workers' security is upset and their work habits are challenged. This anger is a normal and understandable reaction toward something that is unwanted. The feeling cannot be helped, but when the angry feeling is manifested in angry behavior, there is a problem. There are ways to handle anger that keep the problem from escalating.

There is no reason to complicate the work situation by acting on anger. It is essential to acknowledge one's anger and to understand what the anger is all about. The key step then is deciding what to do about the anger. Some people find relief and control in writing about their anger, some use the energy and tension anger generates to accomplish physical work that needs doing. Anger that is channeled can improve performance, such as a better a golf game or harder and faster work. Some anger is best left unexpressed. This strategy works well in work situations. Although anger is legitimate, it is frequently in the employee's best interests to process it internally, rather than rage about it. Anger may be talked out with trusted confidants. Self-talk works if the self-talk is reasonable and dissuades impulsive action. Self-talk that incites more anger is dangerous and counterproductive. But, most of all, managing anger means not taking the changes personally but, understanding the reasons for the changes, and making decisions based on reasoning rather than feelings.

Employees have much in common as they react to change. Rivalry over promotions, competition for attention from the new bosses, or speculation and concern over who gets to keep their job is widespread. It is common to mistrust new employees who are hired by new management, as new employee's attitudes are different from those of older employees who are struggling with change. The new employees adapt to the circumstances as they would to any new job at which they want to do well. Jealousy and dislike toward the new employee's cooperative and enthusiastic attitude is as understandable as it is unfair. Although new employees have a different perspective, they want to be included and compete for the good things the job offers.

Negative emotions require recognition if they are to be harnessed and used in a constructive manner. Raging from anger, withdrawing in frustration, or reacting to fear with paranoia and accusations are not conducive to survival. All employees affected by change experience some or all of these feelings and they tend to react in similar ways. It is, however, unnecessary to be a victim of circumstances and the emotions they may release. There are techniques for survival and ways to become essential to the new bosses and the restructured organization. Change brings losses and gains. Survival is minimizing the former losses and maximizing the latter gains.

SURVIVAL SKILLS

The purpose of this book is to convey strategies for adapting effectively to change. In the chapters that follow, survival skills are enumerated, explained, and examples are given to further illustrate their benefit. Those who use these skills tend to have easier transitions than those who do not. Adaptation is easier than aggravation, more effective than resistance, and more satisfying than fighting. Survival is a healthy and positive goal. Since life is and will always be filled with change, it is better to develop coping strategies and survive than to engage in a losing battle to stop the inevitable.

Kanter (1989) suggests that to survive, employees should make themselves valuable in the entrepreneurial atmosphere of the changing work structure. By pursuing opportunity, taking on more responsibility, developing a variety of skills, staying up to date on pertinent information and emerging needs and markets, setting priorities, working well with coworkers, customers, and suppliers, believing in themselves as job entrepreneurs who can redefine their jobs to meet new needs, and, above all, by constantly learning, employees make themselves essential to the organization. Kanter calls such employees corporate Olympians. They are "focused, fast, friendly, and flexible" (p. 361). This may sound daunting, but it is exciting to know there are ways to deal with the chaos on the job front and emerge not only intact, but with increased skills and marketability. These employees learn and become more valuable because of their experiences. Their abilities and resumes are enhanced and they increase their options.

Employees who survive get themselves noticed by perceiving what needs to be done and suggesting they are the ones to do it. They research the new company, situation, or boss, and with that information in mind explore options that are created because of the resulting change. They recognize their skills and strengths and are self-disciplined (Estess, 1996; Smith, 1996). Survival skills include taking control, making decisions, and creating a good impression, all of which are explored in this book. Employees make their own decisions about their future by looking at options within and outside the company. Options are the basis for feelings of personal and job security and include the development of a special niche in the company and an awareness of what is available to them outside of the company.

Obtaining social support is a survival skill as it offers "stability which protects people in times of transition and stress"

(Ornstein & Sobel, 1987: 126). Survivors look for and get support from their families, any acquaintance who possesses a positive attitude, and from trusted friends and neighbors.

Employees who survive are those who do not deny problems. They may well recognize that the company and the new manager are making ill-advised moves, but they nevertheless work to see positives in the changes and make the changes work for them. Although the boss is not expert in all areas, he or she was hired because someone thought the person had the ability to do what had to be done for the organization to endure. The employee's best interests are served by focusing on what he or she is doing to help himself or herself rather than on what new management is doing that is wrong, unwanted, or has been tried in the past. Employees who are retained do not say it cannot be done, but look at ways to do what must be done. They show respect, are proactive, set a good example, help others, anticipate problems, stay flexible, communicate, and share ideas (Staff, 1997).

All human beings seem to want to hold on to "what is" because it is familiar and comfortable. This, however, prevents problem solving and adaptation to change. The desire is to protect the status quo, but since this cannot be done forever such a strategy ultimately leads to misery as change forces itself in. When change is in fact inevitable, and resistance is strong, emotional turmoil and disorganization result. In contrast, if change is seen as offering possibilities, anxiety becomes excitement and there is room for learning, growing, and hope. It is energizing to think about opportunity (Gerber, 1997).

DECIDE

Alex had complaints about his job and regularly threatened to leave. His relationship with his supervisor was such that he could say, "I quit," without the supervisor taking him seriously and holding him to his word. When the supervisor told Alex he was transferring to another division, he suggested Alex might want to make good on his declarations or stop making them, as the incoming supervisor might believe him. The prospect of lost job security made Alex rethink his attitude. Alex, and other employees throughout the country, must constantly re-evaluate their employment position because of the fluid management situation in today's workplace.

In an era of takeovers, buyouts, reorganizations, rightsizings, downsizings, or whatever the fashionable label of the moment may be, the job climate changes rapidly. Unpredictability is predictable. Workers may either become angry or distressed about this, or they may perceive it as an opportunity and look forward to the change. The change may be an impetus to find a job in another field, open a business, return to school, start a family, take a sabbatical, or look for a better job. Or the change may actually make the company a better place to work or improve the employee's job security by transforming a dwindling business into one that thrives.

The change in management may offer a chance to be recognized for skills and contributions or an opportunity to try out ideas and procedures ignored by previous managers.

Whatever negative or positive changes are anticipated, employees do not reach conclusions in a vacuum. Work changes are accompanied by rumors, unease, mistrust, opinions, and a great deal of talk and speculation. Feelings are influenced by information received from coworkers. Because of the unknown, tension and anxiety are heightened. Feelings are more volatile and easily stirred by the concerns of others. Change is a threat to equilibrium. Change requires adjustments and the achievement of a new balance.

Feelings are more negative when a popular boss is fired, a hostile takeover is engineered, threats of staff reductions are made, or it is suggested the product, procedure, or performance is not up to par.

Obviously, feelings are more positive when a failing business is rescued, there are promises of more money and benefits, increased staffing is expected, or the employment future looks secure.

Employees experiencing the effects of new management—whether they are as mild as policy and procedural changes, or as stinging as employer and employee changes—react to these transitions with strong feelings. Although feelings are expected and are healthy, they can be uncomfortable and spin out of control. It is not helpful to go over and over the same problem with distress and worry. This undermines concentration and the enjoyment of life. It is detrimental to get so angry that hostility and irritability carry over to friends and family. It is damaging to get so depressed that motivation is gone and all hope is lost. It is exhausting to get so anxious that the body responds with fatigue and nervous shaking. It is better to identify feelings and decide what to do about them. This is the first step in surviving new management.

Anxiety is apt to occur in any situation that portends unknown changes. Anxiety is experienced physically as that tense and nervous feeling that includes such symptoms as rapid heart beat, excess sweating, internal shaking, and in extreme cases, temporary amnesia. Unless the reaction is diagnosed as anxiety, people who are unaccustomed to the experience think they are physically sick or falling apart emotionally. It can be so frightening that it is difficult to function effectively. Employees under stress who suffer from anxiety find they can work through the symptoms by staying busy, focusing on their work, and learning that the less they dwell on their symptoms, the quicker the anxiety disappears. Exercise, even something so simple as taking the stairs instead of the elevator, helps to burn off the adrenaline. Deep breathing gets the system back in control. "Square breathing" is even better: Breathe in, counting to four, hold the breath to the count of four, breathe out counting to four, hold the breath to the count of four. This may be repeated several times and used repeatedly throughout the day as needed. Talking to coworkers helps if the focus of the conversation is on the other person. Work at making coworkers comfortable. Get to know them. Make them laugh. The idea is to stay at work, learn that anxiety will go away, and it will go away more quickly if the source of the anxiety is not dwelled upon.

Whenever Maureen felt anxious, she recognized what was happening and distracted herself by throwing paper clips into a cup for a few minutes. The eye-hand coordination requirements of the exercise absorbed all of her concentration and allowed her to relax enough to get back to work in a calmer state of mind.

Worry, the most common reaction to the unknown, is not at all useful to employees suffering stress, unless it results in problem solving. Employees who address their worries by determining what they can reasonably do about the situation and what is beyond their control are taking care of their concerns in a constructive manner. When people get stuck in a state of worry they are unable to solve problems or move on. The same distressing worries go around and around in their minds with no release or relief. If the worrier is convinced that worry is necessary because he or she believes worrying is the responsible thing to do and thinks worry prevents problems, a "worry-time" can be scheduled during which all worries are acknowledged, written down, and worried about at one time. Worries are postponed until the set worry-time occurs and the individual is situated in the worry-place and can spend the next hour concentrating on the worries. Once the time is up, worrying is over until the next day at the appointed time.

Devin was a worrier and found it difficult to give it up. He thought if he did not worry, catastrophes were sure to happen. Since he could not stop worrying, he knew he had to manage his worries so his head was not always full of his self-appointed concerns. He did this by deciding he would not worry about anything that was either not his problem, or anything that was impossible to do anything about. He took on all other worries, but saved them for the end of the day when he spent his hour drive-time concentrating on his problems. Through this method he kept his mind clear at home and at work and also managed to solve some of his dilemmas.

Anger flares when employees feel slighted, are not consulted about changes that affect them, or when the new manager dictates changes that make their work more difficult, their position less prestigious, and their influence negligible. As satisfying as venting justified anger can be, it is nevertheless dangerous if used to fix blame, put others on the defensive, or leads to bitterness that develops into an ongoing resolve to destroy or get even. Employees who recognize their anger can talk themselves out of it by not taking the boss's actions personally, deciding to act rationally and in their own best interests, and settling into a wait-and-see attitude (Hughes, 1993).

Employees want to look good and be appreciated. By managing their emotions in a way that benefits them, this is more likely to occur.

Josselyn was very angry and upset. When she heard the company had been bought by a larger corporation she knew she would lose her job, her health insurance for her family, her car, and her house. She would now have to take her children and go live with her mother. These fears buzzed through her mind until she was a nervous wreck. Expecting the worst, she was irritable and short-tempered. She had struggled long years to be independent and support her family. She had finally found a job she liked where she felt appreciated and made a good living. When all of this seemed to be going up in smoke, her emotions overwhelmed her to the point she was unable to do her work. Fortunately, she recognized this and was able to get herself under control because she knew her anxiety was only making her problem worse. She wrote out her concerns and developed a plan for solving each one. As she put her plan into action her fears became more manageable. Although she was still angry and depressed, she acted pleasant, calm, and happy. The act was good enough for her to appear as though she was in control. The feedback she received from others gave her strength. She buckled down to her job, no longer at the mercy of her emotions. Pretending to be in control resulted in an actual sense of control. Josselyn's first step was accomplished— she had identified her emotions and worked with them until she had mastered them. It was at this point that she began to think rationally about her job.

Deciding whether or not to stick it out is the second major step in surviving new management. This is crucial because adjusting to a work situation that no longer offers the same routine and security is not easy. With change and rumor of change bombarding employees from all directions, it takes a calculated determination to concentrate on one's work. For this reason it is beneficial for workers to know why they want to keep their job. The more convincing and important the reasons, the more likely the employee will keep to his or her course of job survival. The following format helps marshal thoughts. If the answers to the questions are written out or tape-recorded they can be referred to during times of job stress when employees are likely to waiver in their decision to stay on the job. During difficult times it is important for employees to remember why they want to keep their job.

The following example analyzes a change in management from the employee's viewpoint. The answers are made-up to show how the analysis might look. A decision is crucial as employees need reasons to stick tight during the stress of management change. Consequently, knowing why one wants to stay and how to stay are an essential part of the critique.

JOB DECISION WORKSHEET
(Example)

WHAT I LIKE ABOUT THE JOB
1. Only need one car for both of us to go to work.
2. Enjoy the work.
   a. Salary is good.
   b. Feel acceptance and approval.
   c. Every day is interesting.
3. Feel satisfaction in how well I do the job.

WHAT I DISLIKE ABOUT THE JOB
1. Unhappy with one of the other employees.
   a. He shirks his work.
   b. He grumbles all day long.
2. Problem with parking.
3. All work and no play.

WHAT I LIKE ABOUT THE COMPANY
1. Good benefits
2. Offices in many states.

WHAT I DISLIKE ABOUT THE COMPANY
1. Don't fire deadwood.
2. No training opportunities.

WHAT I LIKE ABOUT THE BOSS
1. Listens.
2. Fair.

WHAT I DISLIKE ABOUT THE BOSS
1. Changes her mind a lot.
2. Has no clout with her boss.

CHANGES THAT BENEFIT ME
1. Better office building
2. Chance to suggest some good ideas I've saved.

CHANGES THAT BENEFIT THE COMPANY
1. Better leadership.
2. New ideas and goals.

HOW A CHANGE IN MANAGEMENT BENEFITS ME
1. Get to start with a clean slate.

HOW A CHANGE IN MANAGEMENT HURTS ME
1. Have to start all over to establish a reputation.

JOB DECISION WORKSHEET
(Example Continued)

WHAT I CONTRIBUTE TO THE COMPANY

1. I've been one of the top 10 earners for the past five years.
2. I plan the annual holiday celebration.
3. I was a key liaison person during the last merger.
4. I can work with anybody.
5. I can finish assignments fast when speed is required.
6. I am cross-trained and can do several different jobs.

ASSETS THAT MAKE ME A VALUABLE EMPLOYEE

1. I have 10 years of experience.
2. I arrive on time and stay late if the work requires it.
3. I get along well with coworkers, suppliers, and customers.
4. I am willing and in fact like to learn new things.
5. I am able to help the new boss and the new employees.

HOW EASILY CAN I BE REPLACED?

1. There are many people available who have the same training I have; however, it is hard to find someone with the combination of skill and work experience I have.

MY WORST FEARS ARE

1. I will be fired.
2. I will be laid off.
3. I will not be included in decision making or consulted regarding changes that affect me and my job.
4. I won't be able to do the job the new manager assigns me.
5. I will be criticized and embarrassed in front of others.

WHAT ARE THE RUMORS?
ARE THEY REALISTIC?

RUMORS	FACTS
1. Everyone will be replaced.	1. Not very likely. Someone has to do the work in the meantime.
2. The new boss is bringing all his own people.	2. Possibly some, but not all. Someone has to teach them about the company.
3. Everybody will get pay cuts and benefit reductions.	3. Possible. Probably not, as salaries here are in line with the rest of the industry.

DO I WANT TO KEEP MY JOB?

Yes.

WHY DO I WANT TO KEEP MY JOB?

1. I am vested in the retirement plan.
2. Other jobs in my field are hard to find.
3. I like my work.
4. I don't want to leave the community.
5. My family is established here.

WHAT CAN I DO TO KEEP MY JOB?

1. Offer to help new management and employees.
2. Let new management know what I am doing now that contributes to the company.
3. Continue to be a reliable and responsible employee.
4. Let the new boss know I am willing to work with him.
5. Find out what new directions are planned and help the company achieve the goals.
6. Help the company leaders establish themselves in the community.
7. Be positive.

During the process of management shifts, information changes daily. Employees' ideas and evaluations change as new information surfaces. Writing out or tape-recording the analysis and changing it as circumstances change, gives individuals organized knowledge that they would not otherwise have in such a state of upheaval. The recorder is advised to include humorous incidents as humor is in short supply during periods of transition.

New management initiates a murky situation. Analysis, decision, and direction make it less so. People who know what they want have a leg up. They do not have to continually reevaluate.

The following is a review of one worker's summary:

Steve liked his job as a salesman in a software company because he was gaining experience. He saw people struggling with all kinds of problems and was constantly learning. He was hired right out of school and was grateful to be given the chance. He felt respected by his coworkers and enjoyed being with them. They shared experiences, were supportive, and acquired knowledge from each other. His home was not far from work. His wife had a job she liked in the area. His children were doing well in school.

But Steve had some dissatisfaction with the status quo. He felt the administration was too conservative and authoritative. He disliked the fact that everyone seemed to know each other's private business. He thought management should instigate new, progressive methods of research so that the company could stay ahead of its competitors. He knew the company needed better publicity and needed to be more responsive to the customers' preferences. He had ideas, but they were rejected because his present boss was satisfied with the way things were.

When Steve learned there would be a merger, he was pleased because he saw it as an opportunity for progress. He figured there would be a more proactive stance in regard to the product and the demands of the public. He was ready to fall in line with whatever new ideas and actions would be enacted. Although Steve did not have much experience, he knew he could contribute because he was sure he shared the new management's philosophy. He hoped his enthusiasm would compensate for his meager work experience. Because he endorsed change, he thought he would be a valued employee, even though he recognized he could be replaced by another recent graduate. Steve's major fear was that the new boss would bring in his own people or hire employees who could better implement his own sense of mission.

Steve's coworkers were apprehensive. They talked with people who worked with the new boss and heard he picked favorites, relied on them, and shut out the rest of the employees. They heard he was disorganized and power hungry. But Steve heard he was good at getting support for what he wanted and was interested in matching the product with needs. He appeared energetic and acted as though he wanted acceptance. Steve did not know what to believe. But he knew that his coworkers' fear was based on conjecture, not fact, and he decided to wait and assess the boss's character for himself. He knew he wanted to keep his job. He needed more work experience and besides, did not want to upset his family. He thought the business could be turned around. He threw his support behind the new boss and hoped that would help him keep his job. He hoped that when the boss understood he was interested in helping him adjust to the new position he would not feel he had to look elsewhere for a good employee.

Steve knew he had a contribution to make. His inner life was less chaotic because of his resolute decision. He knew what he wanted. He planned to tell his new boss he could be of value to him, to the organization, and to the customers (Carr & Fletcher, 1990).

Steve and his coworkers were often unhappy with the prospective changes, lack of security, and the unsettling gossip, but Steve had a way to manage the stress. He recorded his feelings, recognized the rumors to be just that, and reminded himself to work only with the facts as he knew them. This helped him maintain his equilibrium. Because of his unclouded vision, he adapted, kept his job, and became an important member of the software company. He made contributions and was rewarded for his work. He was satisfied with his decision and glad he made the effort to stay through the unsettling change process. Not everyone in the company made the same decision as Steve. Several employees left for other jobs, one retired, another was fired, hired a labor lawyer, and engaged in a long, expensive court battle which the employee lost. Some employees were demoted, others promoted, and almost all were shifted to other jobs or had their job descriptions changed. By the end of the first year of new management Steve and his coworkers who were also determined to keep their jobs had adjusted to the new boss, the new policies, and met many new people they liked and found they could work with them.

New management is change and change is threatening and stressful, particularly when it causes financial worry. But there is a way to survive, in fact not just survive but prevail. It begins with recognizing and managing emotions and making a decision about whether or not to hang in for the long run.

There are decisions to make:
1. Decide whether or not to stay with the company.
2. Remember the reasons for the decision.
3. Do not ignore the negative but focus on the positive.
4. See change as opportunity.

CHAPTER ONE REVIEW

1. What are the pros and cons of staying with the company and working with new management?
2. Does what the job offers make it worthwhile to stay and cope with change?
3. Is the situation such that the employee is better off to stay?
4. Have techniques been developed for remembering precisely why the employee wants to keep the job?

CHAPTER 2

TAKE CARE OF YOURSELF

Angela did not like surprises. She had a hard time adjusting to alterations in her routine, and was comfortable with the status quo. She had a good working relationship with her boss and knew her job. Her anxiety about new management increased as her fears and apprehensions intensified. Luckily, she recognized the problem as her own and knew she had to help herself if her transition to a new boss was going to work. Her old boss was gone and her ongoing adjustment depended on her actions and attitude. Yes, change was hard, but she decided that leaving would be even harder.

The new boss, the job, the salary, and the benefits are important, but nothing deserves higher priority than the individual struggling to survive. If employees do not take care of themselves, they cannot take care of their jobs.

A change in administration never seems to come at a convenient time. It often coincides with other life pressures, such as sick family members, marital problems, personal difficulties, or social setbacks. It is part of the way life is and not a conspiracy designed to complicate people's lives. There is no perfect time for change to happen.

Let's face it: Employment problems put a damper on any life. What happens because of corporate manipulation is beyond the power of the employee, but what happens to the individual is in large part within his or her control. Attitude and determination are make-or-break factors. Employees may hate what is happening, but can take charge of how it affects them (Viscott, 1977). Although the job situation has been thrown into confusion because of the onslaught of change, the self can be salvaged because whatever happens on the job does not change who a person is. If the employee has talents, abilities, friends, support from relatives, and respect from coworkers, those life components persist. Changes at work do not change those circumstances. If workers hold on to what they have, and see work as only one aspect of life, they are better able to tolerate change. Change does not have to dominate one's entire life, even though job insecurities may cause old insecurities to surface. The insecurities can be managed by seeing the new experiences as challenges which present a chance to grow and learn. Resulting skills include better stress and life management, compassion and understanding for other people going through similar problems, and preparation for future life changes.

TACTIC # 1: BE CIRCUMSPECT

Amy's problem-solving style was to discuss her concerns with everyone within range of her voice. She did not silently ponder her troubles or read up on possible approaches and solutions. She was excitable, verbally demanding, and wanted people to listen and respond. One discussion was not enough. She re-assessed her distress from all possible angles, day after day. She wondered why people gave her pat advice, cut her off saying she had already told them all about it, or kept glancing at the clock. One worn-out listener told her to stop using the "splatter" approach and settle down to organize and think through her thoughts. She wanted discussion, but took this advice from an irritated coworker and was more discriminating about what she said to whom.

Of course, people want to talk to others about job problems, but discrimination is the key word. Holding all the stress inside is not necessary, but it is necessary to select tolerant, trusted people as confidants.

Coworkers share similar experiences and are at the front lines of the stress. It is easy to discuss problems with them, but not always wise. Their concerns may be so alarming that their distress is infectious. Troubled thoughts are not helped by further laments.

Employees have friends and family members who are intimately involved with their job problems. Friends and family members care and want their loved ones to be happy and content. They are happy to listen and give advice. However, if complaints and concerns persist they become more desperate in trying to help as they do not like to see people they care about suffer. They resort to the fix-it approach, offering the distressed employee a range of advice that may or may not be useful, such as confront the boss, forget it, go along with new management, or quit the job. When employees realize their friends and relatives have grown tired of hearing about the persistent job problems, alienation may set in on both sides. Anger is a side affect that complicates emotions. Friends and relatives get angry because they cannot seem to help and the troubled employees get upset because people do not want to listen to them anymore.

If the employees have completed the first two survival steps by acknowledging their emotions and deciding how to manage them and making a decision about keeping their jobs, they are better able to be circumspect about their distresses. They can refrain from agitating and turning people off with their job concerns. Support is wanted and needed. Driving people away by asking them to do something they cannot do is counterproductive. An employee's bad times do not have to be a bad time for everyone involved. Relatives do care and want to know what is going on, but can be told in a way that lets them know the workers are making a good effort to handle their problems. Workers help their families through difficult times by taking control and maintaining their own effectiveness.

Employees are circumspect when they take advice under advisement, using only what helps them achieve their goal of staying employed. They are circumspect when they stop dwelling on the negatives. If negatives are emphasized, negative thinking predominates. Employees already know what they like and do not like. All that was considered when they made their decision to keep their job (Carnegie, 1951).

Trish was not circumspect. She felt out of control and thought the new boss was trying to get rid of her. She was angry and depressed and her self-confidence was depleted. She listened and reacted to all the rumors and was in a constant state of agitation. Each night she told her husband the gory details. He listened and was sympathetic and encouraging. As her reports became more paranoid (she was sure everything that happened was aimed at her), he tried to reassure her and explain that the changes were just changes and had nothing to do with her. She accused him of disloyalty and of failing to be supportive. As he tried to be objective and evaluate the information, she became more impatient. She decided he was not there for her when she needed him, was not on her side, and they should not be together. He was not enjoying their relationship either because his needs were not considered and he was apparently unable to help her, so he agreed. Because Trish did not make a decision about what she wanted and was not circumspect, she lost her major source of support and developed another distressing problem.

Aaron could not bring himself to ignore the talk at work because he wanted to know what was going on. However, he did not repeat the gossip to others and weighed it against his decision to keep his job. He kept his family updated, but did not alarm them needlessly. He shared some of his frustrations and worries with them, but he did so in such a way as to let them know he was evaluating, accepting, and coping. They knew of his desire to stay employed in his present position. They also knew he felt his security was threatened. But they did not feel that his emotions were out of control or that they had to intervene to keep him from doing something foolish. The family relationship continued to be strong and supportive.

Being circumspect requires the following steps:
1. Keep job goals in mind.
2. Get thoughts organized.
3. Find a trusted listener.
4. Talk regularly to persons who are trustworthy.
5. Once an issue is settled do not keep going over it.
6. Use input from trusted sources to help solve problems and make decisions.

TACTIC # 2: MAINTAIN DIGNITY

Oscar was ready to grovel to keep his job. In fact, he did grovel, but hated himself for doing it. He felt he would rather lose his job than continue that way. He knew he had to do something different.

It is hard to maintain dignity when new people show no respect for the company history, the development of the product, and the contributions of the workers. As frustrating as this is, dwelling on it only develops negative emotions, and prevents assimilation of new people, policies, and procedures. New management is there to bring in the new. They are there to propose changes. Their actions are not directed at the old workers. There is no reason to take their actions as personal assaults. Managers simply want the employees to carry out the proposed changes. Each are there to do their jobs.

It is possible to maintain dignity by remembering the good work one has done. Everyone in the company has performed services of value and meaning, or the company would not exist for new management to manage. New directions mean different directions, not a right or wrong course of action. Employees who have been with the company have specialized experience and knowledge to offer. There is dignity in that special status (McGarvey, 1990).

Change is not a foreign element in anybody's life. The company and the people who work for it have already experienced a great deal of change throughout their working lives. The changes may have been incremental, but they were changes nonetheless, and employees adjusted and incorporated them into their work lives without feeling threatened. Mild aggravation was probably the major symptom. If the changes new management bring are accepted and integrated into the employee's workstyle there is no need to feel disloyal to the past or afraid of the future. If the changes are seen as part of the continuum of change, dignity is maintained. If one can accept changes without resistance and with an open mind, one will be a better and more efficient employee. If a worker fights new procedures with defiance he or she will not be able to adapt effectively to change. Dignity works, defiance does not.

Dignity is maintained through the implementation of a matter-of-fact, straight-forward manner. Employees can be courteous and cooperative, friendly and helpful, and keep their self-respect.

Customers do not have to know there is trouble in the company. Worries and dissatisfaction are the worker's personal domain. Sharing them with customers or other business contacts is not dignified. It does not help the employee and is troublesome to the customers. Complaining makes the employee sound pitiful and the customer is all too happy to take his or her business elsewhere.

Janice liked her job and the financial security it afforded. She was terrified her position would be eliminated. To make sure that this did not happen, she kept up her usual good work. However, she feared this might not be enough. She decided she had to go out of her way to endear herself to her new boss. She gave compliments, reported office gossip, and brought goodies from home. To make points, she verbally compared the new boss favorably with the old one. She hated herself for taking this approach. Although she pretended to be cheerful and enthusiastic at work, she was morose and irritable at home. She had to admit that if it took what she was doing to keep her job, the job was not worth it. She felt undignified, phony, a false friend to those in the office who confided in her. She could not continue her charade so she made a change. She remained cheerful and enthusiastic, but turned her cheer and enthusiasm on her work. She ceased trying to win over her boss with compliments and gossip and went back to concentrating on doing a good job. As it happened, her job was eliminated. But she was recognized as a good worker and offered another position within the company, which meant a transfer to another department. She took it, liked it, and kept it. Whenever she was insecure or felt pressure to endear herself to a boss she reminded herself of this experience and kept her dignity.

Richard liked his work, but was unhappy with new management's decision to introduce a new reporting system. He hated working with the new and, to him, more complicated forms. But he had to do it as he got paid by the number of people he saw—no report, no pay. Consequently, he busied himself gathering the information. However, he did not make the transition smoothly. As he accustomed himself to the requirements, he complained to his contacts. Soon the agency was getting feedback from them that they should be more concerned about people and put less emphasis on paper. Since the complaints came from people who worked with Richard, his new employers had no trouble figuring out who caused the sudden rash of grievances. Richard was in trouble. He was a good employee and kept his job, but not without a warning. He learned to maintain his professional dignity while he dealt with the unpleasant aspects of the job. He stopped troubling the company's customers with his troubles.

Steps to dignity are:

1. Acknowledge accomplishments.
2. Accept the inevitability of change.
3. Be helpful and cooperative, not subservient and groveling.
4. Maintain a business-like demeanor in all business contacts.

TACTIC # 3: WORK ON APPEARANCE AND STYLE

Francine took a lot of sick leave. She earned it and felt she deserved to take it when she got tired, stayed out late, or thought she needed a "mental health day." If she did come in on a bad day she did not look at all well. She was unnecessarily complicating her life. Francine had a problem because she was not giving her job the priority it deserved. Old or new management has a problem with this type of behavior, but old management may be more tolerant if the employee has been on the job and performed satisfactorily over a period of time.

Brant was a nice guy, but alarming in appearance. His hair was seldom trimmed and he shaved irregularly. His shoes were not shined. He did not wear socks. He looked like an unmade bed. When he saw how the transition team members dressed he decided he was going to have to do something about his appearance. In Brant's case, the advent of new management probably saved his career. He wasn't going anywhere with old management because of the way he presented himself.

New management sees employees as a package. The package is made up of skills, ability, personality, potential, and appearance. If one of the elements is missing, such as appearance, the package is not as desirable. Every employee has the opportunity to look good. New management does not hold them back from looking as good as they can.

Making a favorable appearance is an asset for any worker. Not only does it make a good impression, but it brings good feedback, which leads to good feelings. Looking good and feeling good are worthwhile in any endeavor. Looking good enhances self-confidence and puts emphasis on the most important person in everyone's life, himself or herself.

Dress style is dictated by the type of business and the requirements of the company. Some establishments have detailed dress codes. Some provide uniforms and insist on a uniform appearance. Employees who want to keep their job conform to the mandates of management. Observe the style of the company's leaders and model dress choices after them. Creativity is a good thing, but not if it leads to outlandish or zany clothes. Employees represent the company and management notes whether or not they look the part (Horton, 1992). Not knowing how to dress or claiming poverty are inadequate excuses for not conforming. Employees can get help from people who do know or go to specialists who are paid to style hair, select flattering colors, and suggest appropriate styles. Those in financial duress can shop thrift shops for great bargains.

Dottie's chip-on-the-shoulder attitude was that what new administration saw is what they got. This is an example of what not to do. She decided that she was who she was and she wasn't going to change for anyone. They could get used to her. These are brave, but unwise words.

Companies have their own styles. Construction workers, repair people, and house painters, for example, are not expected to be as neat at the end of the day as they are at the beginning. But everyone who works inside and does not deal with materials that emit dirt and residue is expected to be presentable from the beginning to the end of the work day. Employees may express their individual styles at home and while pursuing personal pleasures, but while on work premises and while representing the company they need to dress and act as a representative of the firm. One of the easiest and most obvious adjustments a new or old employee can make is to look the part by dressing according to new management's expectations. There is nothing like a new situation for taking stock and making improvements in appearance.

Another style which new management takes note of is that of work habits. Everyone has his or her own working style whether they are new to the business or have been at it for years. Work styles can also be adjusted to match the needs of the new boss. Some bosses like verbal reports on a regular basis. Others prefer written reports at the end of a project. Is the boss casual and friendly or formal and all business? Adopt the style that works best with his or her personality. If employees want to stay on the job they can market themselves as a product that will satisfy the expectations of the new boss (Calano & Salzman, 1988).

Change may be minimal or immense, depending on the circumstances of the change. A new boss promoted from within a going concern may make minor changes. A boss recruited to turn a company around has a mission that necessitates major changes. Big trouble in the company means big changes. Employees adjust to the change or adjust to joblessness. If there is a decision to stay, there is a decision to change (Garfield, 1992).

If new management's style is contrary to the employee's style, it is harder, but not impossible, to adapt. The following is a check list to help employees compare and contrast their styles to new management's. It may take some time to decide how new management prefers to work, but this list makes it possible to key in on important work style issues.

WORK STYLE CHECK LIST

[Place a X next to each statement that represents new management's style and an O next to each statement that represents your personal style.]

____ Casual	____ Formal
____ Disorganized	____ Organized
____ Talks out problems	____ Talks after decisions are made
____ Prefers few directives	____ Prefers a clear set of directives
____ Wants someone else to make the decisions	____ Wants to make the decisions
____ Likes to work with a team	____ Likes to work alone
____ Prefers to work with people	____ Prefers to work with paper
____ Likes busy, bustling, noisy workplace	____ Likes quiet surroundings
____ Likes new challenges	____ Likes a familiar routine
____ Orderly workplace not important	____ Wants everything in its place
____ Wants to give the orders	____ Wants to be given orders
____ Doesn't want to be told what to do	____ Appreciates instructions
____ Self-starter	____ Wants to be told when to do it
____ Works well without supervision	____ Needs work checked regularly
____ Wants personal involvement with coworkers	____ Wants to keep work relationships at work
____ Works well under pressure	____ Dislikes emergencies and unexpected work
____ Likes to be noticed	____ Likes privacy

Delores was a whiz at forecasting economic trends. The people she worked with knew that and did not care that she wore jeans, never had her hair styled, and ate breakfast at her desk. The new managers were not so dependent on her skills. They looked at the whole package as they decided who to keep and who to let go. Delores's sloppy appearance made them wonder if she had the right stuff. After all, she was not the only economic analyzer in the world. Since Delores was interested in her work and not interested in personal appearance, it did not occur to her that she would be judged on anything other than her ability to make an important work contribution. She was shocked and angry when she heard she was among the employees who might be out-placed. But she knew she wanted the job, so she put her anger aside and asked a trusted friend what she thought the problem might be. The friend was candid. Delores found it unsettling, but decided she could do something about it. She asked for help and responded to direction. She found easy-to-wear clothes that helped her appear to be the dedicated business woman she was. She had her hair styled in an attractive, easy-to-care-for fashion. She agreed to wear a touch of lipstick. She looked and felt great. She wished she had done this years before. She kept her job.

Howard looked super. He was tuned into appearance and knew how to dress to look his best. Since how he looked meant a lot to him, he devoted attention to the details of his grooming and attire. When he thought he had it right he felt splendid. This feeling gave Howard the edge he needed to keep his job.

Lois reported every move to her boss. She dropped in and discussed her actions in detail. Her style did not match the boss's style. He saw people by appointment, communicated by writing memos, and was interested in final results. If she had paid attention she could have saved herself the embarrassment of having to listen to her boss point out her style as an example of how not to work with him.

Jean worked for a boss who did not trust any of the employees to function independently and responsibly without close supervision. Since she did not realize this, she did not reassure him of her dependable work habits. He cut back her hours because he thought she was goofing off. She was angry and insulted, but not too upset to do what was necessary. She took time to observe the boss and determine what he wanted. Then she made sure he knew she was hard at work. She worked herself back into a full-time job.

Adapt appearance and style to new management:

1. Take an appearance inventory.
2. Look the part.
3. Do what it takes to make a good impression.
4. Understand that new management means a new style.
5. Determine what changes are necessary.
6. Change styles to adapt.

TACTIC # 4: PRACTICE STRESS ALLEVIATION

Cameron was not worried about new management because he confidently sailed through everything. This was his first job after graduation. He liked it and thought he was doing well. He did not understand the stress of change and insecurity in the workplace because he had never experienced it. When he found he was under scrutiny and was expected to adjust to a different work style, he did not know how to handle himself. He was falling apart and needed to learn to manage stress—and fast.

Anyone who has ever been through a change in management understands the intensity of this stress. Stress is part of everyday life and everyone has experienced it in some form or another. People, however, are not equally skilled at managing stress. Those who have learned how to handle stress from former experiences have an advantage over those who think they can do nothing about stress.

Stress is worse during times of trauma, loss, uncertainty, and change. Stress symptoms manifest themselves physically, emotionally, and behaviorally. All people do not have all the possible stress symptoms. They may even have unique symptoms not common among the majority of stress sufferers. The following symptoms are indicative of stress.

Mental

*Anxiety   Depression   Poor concentration
Forgetfulness   Weariness   Hopelessness
Helplessness   Anger   Panic   Worry   Fear
Poor self-esteem   Lack of self-confidence*

Physical

*Headaches   Stomach upsets   Tension
Rapid heart beat   Chills   Sweats
Blurred vision   Cold hands and feet
Backaches   Sore muscles
Increased incidences of colds and respiratory
problems*

Behavioral

*Sleeping problems   Eating problems
Irritability   Crying   Inability to control temper
Hyperactivity   Withdrawal and isolation*

Since chronic health problems flair up during times of sustained stress, medical attention may be necessary.

Stress reactions are normal in stressful situations and techniques are available to help one manage and reduce stress. Some effective methods follow.

Relaxation

Relaxation techniques are as individual as stress reactions. Some people go into a trance staring at television. It blocks out everything else and they relax. It is, however, not popular with family members who appreciate responsiveness and attention. Other ways to relax include listening to music, social conversations, movies, watching the waves roll in (Dyer, 1980), meditation, deep breathing, or warm baths.

Deep breathing is the basis for any relaxation exercise. People who have trouble relaxing find deep breathing helps them achieve a state of repose that is effective for them. Tension from stress causes shallow breathing, which is reversed with deep breathing. Anyone who finds relaxation impossible can find help by deep breathing and practicing muscle control five or ten minutes a day. It does not take long to get the hang of it.

Progressive Relaxation

1. Get in a comfortable position.
2. Concentrate on each body part as it is tensed and relaxed.
3. Progress through each body part, from the toes to the forehead.
4. Speak directly to each body part, tensing and then relaxing it.
5. For example: Tense the toes. Let them relax, saying, "Relax toes, relax more." Tense the feet. Let them relax, saying, "Relax feet, relax more."
6. Tense and relax every part of the body.
7. Before stopping make a quick survey of the body and relax those parts that are tense.
8. Continue to relax for up to 20 minutes.

Once proficient in this technique, relaxation comes easily as the body learns to take instruction from the mind. Relaxation tapes and videos are for sale at book and video stores and may also be helpful.

Quick Relaxation

The "Quickie" can be used repeatedly, anywhere, anytime, and is a convenient technique for quick relaxation during a stressful work day.

1. Take a deep breath and say, "Alert mind, calm body."
2. Let the neck and shoulders sag.
3. Smile (grin, not grim) and take another deep breath.
4. Go about the business of the day.

Relaxation tapes and videos can be bought at book and video stores.

Michelle was an active, driven woman. She could not picture herself relaxing. Nevertheless, she needed a way to cope with the constant stress she felt while trying to adjust to changes at work. She tried a few deep breaths. That worked. She followed up by relaxing her neck and shoulders. That worked too. She used relaxation to get her through her busy day. When she got home she set her timer for five minutes, took a few deep breaths, and pictured herself in a calm, peaceful place. She picked a mountain trail. She became so adept at relaxation, she had only to picture the mountain and she immediately felt unburdened and at peace.

Exercise

Exercise is useful for burning off the accumulated adrenaline and other chemicals that build up in the system during times of stress. Exercise helps the body manufacture endorphins which contribute to a feeling of well-being. Exercise includes sports, bike riding, walking, aerobics, skating, weight training, swimming, jumping rope, or any activity that involves physical exertion for up to 20 minutes a day. Exercising pays off in stress reduction and is regularly recommended for health maintenance.

Elaine's idea of exercise was a walk from her chair to the refrigerator during a commercial. However, her tension at work became so pronounced that good food, eaten regularly, was not enough. She bought a jumping rope to use during TV commercials. She lost both weight and tension.

Distraction

The human mind cannot concentrate on two things at one time. Consequently, distraction is a great stress reliever. Playing with the children, reading an action-packed book, crafts, fishing, playing a musical instrument, or working a puzzle are good distractions. Finding a distraction that is pleasurable is doubly beneficial. Linda enjoyed sewing. It demanded her undivided attention and she was proud of the finished project. There were three successes (enjoyment, distraction, achievement) in her stress relief project.

Talking About It

Discussing problems gets them out into the light of day. This alone helps dispel them or puts them in a different "light." Once the problems are heard by the speaker there is a better chance that they can be solved, dismissed, or even seen to be humorous. If a good listener is not available or if there is no one trustworthy around, the problems can be written down. Talking or writing helps organize thoughts and brings relief from the burden of holding the distress inside or pretending that all is well.

Rodney did not like to share his problems with anybody. He was brought up to believe that people who talked about problems were weak and vulnerable. As his concerns about work increased, so did his silence. He had sleeping problems, his stomach hurt, and he found himself withdrawing. He felt and looked terrible and was developing problems at home; everyone thought he was angry at them and did not know why. After one particularly trying day he went home, exploded with anger over some trivial incident, and ended up having a heart-to-heart with his wife. Her concern and question was, "Why didn't you tell me before?" That night Rodney slept well. After that, when his wife asked him about his day he had an answer for her.

Self-talk

There is not always someone available for discussion. Self-talk is necessary when this is the case. It is also a good technique for controlling anger, anxiety, and other emotional reactions. Self-talk is a person's own reassuring voice encouraging moderate behavior, explaining for example, the other person's reasons for indiscriminate verbal attacks. It helps one to acknowledge feelings. Self-talk is essential for staying sane through crazy times, when the boss's actions enrage and demean, or when insecurity strikes. Self-talk helps individuals get through tough situations by delaying action, taking time to evaluate, and not reacting to other people's personal problems.

Stephanie was a reactor. She bragged that no one ever got the upper hand with her. If she did not like something, she was direct in her response. This worked well with the past administration at her place of work because they appreciated her honesty. Since she frequently was the person who spoke up, spoke up immediately, and spoke for the employee group, the former administration got the feedback they needed and wanted when changes were contemplated. Not so with the new administration. Even her toned-down reactions were more than they wanted to hear. They saw their mission as effecting change that would alter the course of the company and save it from bankruptcy. They wanted cooperation, not complaints. Stephanie had to learn to react silently and talk herself through her feelings (Helmstetter, 1987). She managed by reminding herself that the administration was concerned about saving the company. However they did it was good for her and her coworkers. She recognized they could not take her personal preferences into consideration. She took their actions under advisement and evaluated the changes in the light of long term gains and goals.

Steps to stress alleviation are:
1. Admit that stress and change are inevitable.
2. Identify stress points.
3. Notice where stress is taking its toll.
4. Learn and practice stress alleviation activities.

TACTIC # 5: PRACTICE PREVENTIVE HEALTH MEASURES

When Connie's stomach problems started acting up she took notice. She learned that her coworkers were also suffering from chronic health problems due to the stress of change. She immediately got herself on a good health regimen and advised her friends to do the same.

The stress of change requires good health. The better the health, the better the chance of success in circumstances that require extra stamina. Adjusting to a new boss necessitates a more than normal output of effort because vigilance and tension are by-products of new and unknown conditions. Preventive health care to forestall sickness and good health practices to maintain health are recommended at any time, but particularly during times of prolonged stress. In psychologist Maslow's description of the hierarchy of needs, physical needs are listed as the most basic (Lawless, 1973). When the body talks, listen.

Taking care of health needs is important. It is just as important to avoid sharing personal health needs with the new boss. New management wants producers. If the supervisor is given any reason to think that any of the personnel is not up to doing the job, their work will be observed with that in mind. Management has to worry about production, insurance costs, workman's compensation payments, and company liability. Of course, if the employee's health problems are already known, they cannot be denied, but they can be minimized. A frank talk may be in order if the boss needs reassurance that health will not stand in the way of the work.

It is easy for people to put their own health needs on the back burner when more crucial concerns are at hand. This is not wise. Good health is a priority in any circumstance and particularly during stressful times. Self-neglect occurs when worries mount. Depression over unwanted change may lead to a "who cares" or "what's the use" attitude. This can cause further unhealthy actions such as eating or drinking too much or taking unnecessary risks. When people feel they are put upon, emotionally bereft, and are not getting the rewards they deserve, they tend to indulge in pursuits that complicate matters rather than make them better. Partying all night, trying to work with a hangover, eating foods that induce health problems, or engaging in behaviors that are dangerous or illegal are not good for a person's health and produce unneeded additional problems.

Uncomplicating life with healthy activities is good for a person both on and off the job. Rewarding healthy behaviors with a health club membership, a walk, an extra hour of sleep, a dinner out, lunch with friends, a knock-out outfit, a spectator sport, or a good movie are healthy and productive.

The stress of work is a poor excuse to do more of what is not good for the health. Smoking, drinking, and drugs are all in this category. The pretext that a time of stress is not a good time to give up a bad habit is a bad defense. What better time is there to give up bad habits? New management causes employees to feel a loss of control, while giving up a bad health habit gives them control in an area where they have ultimate control. It is a healthy step emotionally and physically.

As pressures at work mounted, Teresa smoked more cigarettes. Since her resistance was already low because of the stress of change she came down with a cold that refused to leave. She went to see a physician. She was bluntly told that she was going to suffer continued colds and respiratory problems unless she stopped smoking. She said she could not quit because she was going through a difficult time at work. Her doctor explained that she would have problems at work whether or not she smoked, but she would have problems in every area of her life if she continued smoking and kept getting physically sick. Teresa decided that overcoming her addiction was worth the effort. She survived the management change and the loss of her cigarettes. She looks back at that time as an important juncture in her life. She learned she could manage a major change without her tobacco crutch. The victory convinced her she was a strong person.

Ralph took the change at work hard. He felt in jeopardy. He worked long hours and skipped lunch. He worked at home, neglecting exercise and any personal pleasure. He worked into the night and deprived himself of sleep. Did his self-sacrifice and self-neglect benefit him? He kept his job, but got a divorce and developed a heart problem. Would that have happened anyway? Perhaps, but chances are his behavior contributed to these problems.

Steps to healthy living:
1. Listen to the body.
2. Eat right, exercise, get enough sleep.
3. Do not overindulge in risk-taking behaviors, addictive substances, or work.
4. Take care of health problems and minimize their existence.

CHAPTER TWO REVIEW

1. Is what others say evaluated in the light of personal and professional goals?
2. Are negative people avoided?
3. Are skills and talents recognized?
4. Are coping techniques available and being used?
5. Is the job being done in the way it should be?
6. Is appearance appropriate for the workplace?
7. Does professional attire and grooming make a good first impression?
8. Are stress alleviation techniques understood and practiced?
9. Is a healthy lifestyle a priority?
10. Are chronic health problems addressed?

CHAPTER 3

MONITOR JOB PERFORMANCE

Katrina was of the opinion that if the new managers did not look out for her, she would not look out for them. She acted out her resentment by neglecting her work. Soon she had no work.

Surviving new management requires a many faceted approach which starts with self-care and includes care of the boss, the job, the coworkers, and the organization. All demand continual attention all of the time. There is no one thing to do first.

This is not as complicated and exacting as it sounds. Self-care is an ongoing habit. Then it is a matter of giving attention where attention is needed by tuning into the boss's sensibility, staying abreast with what is going on in the company, and matching work priorities and goals with those of the boss.

TACTIC # 6: CONCEPTUALIZE NEW DIRECTIONS

Ian took one day at a time, and this outlook helped him through much of the stress of new management and new directions. But it did not help him prepare for new expectations.

New bosses have new goals. Responsiveness to these new goals includes acknowledging them and integrating them into the work process. Many people, on and off the job, resist change, trying to keep the old by fitting what they are doing into new ways without making changes. If changes are minimal this may work, but more often people who do this are seen as dinosaurs. In contrast, workers who embrace new ideas and help the boss plan the steps to reach goals are seen as being in sync (Ruch, 1958).

Ginger liked her work. The company was successful and so was she. Then a new boss arrived and talked about acquiring new product lines. Ginger did not take his ideas seriously. It would blow over, she surmised. Why tinker with anything that is working well? Ginger did not move ahead into new areas and was increasingly left out. She thought she was taking good care of her job by holding on to a good thing but in the end was left without a job. If Ginger had tuned in she would not have been turned out.

It upset Celeste if she had to detour on her way to work or change her brand of toothpaste. She simply had a hard time integrating change into her routine. Her uncertainty about a new boss was magnified because of her rigid frame of reference. Since she wanted to keep her job, she decided to ask for direction and do as she was told. If Celeste could do it, anybody can do it.

No one can get where they want to go if they do not know where they are going. Frankly, it is not always easy to find the way when there is a new boss. But it makes no sense to follow an unknown course. If workers are to make their goals coincide with those of new management, they need direction. One way to determine the way is to ask for guidance.

Employees can start by checking if the boss wants them to continue doing what they are doing. Getting the attention of the busy new boss can be a challenge, so verifying whether or not to continue as before may necessitate making an appointment and writing out a report. The boss may have to study what the employee is proposing to determine if it fits in with the grand plan. Although this seems tedious, it is more burdensome for employees to redo work, find out they are doing something someone else is also doing, or learn that the boss is planning to go in an altogether different direction and wants to assign a team to the effort.

Requests for help, guidance, or verification of efforts are well received when they are genuine and sincere. Requests that put the boss on the spot, that are designed to embarrass him or her, or that are aimed at glorifying the employee are transparent and unappealing.

Neil's problem had defied solution for years. He decided to use it to challenge the new boss. To his chagrin and amazement, the boss said he had run into problems like this and had some ideas on how to handle it. Neil had an answer for each proposal: They'd already tried it; it was too expensive; there was no one who could do it; the customers would not accept it. It was clear Neil would not find any suggestion acceptable. The new boss was not impressed.

Not only could Neil have learned from the boss, but he might have used the opportunity to suggest ideas the former management had not wanted to use. Because there is new management, there is new opportunity. This view of new management improves the attitude, lends excitement and interest, and gives the job new meaning. Change is more acceptable when it encompasses changes employees want. Instead of being thrust into a new situation, the workers who have suggestions and ideas are an active part of the change. Bosses like to see employee involvement because they know that this is what makes a new plan work (Mills, 1984).

Employees can jar themselves out of the status quo and into a creative mode by pretending they have never done the job before and thinking through each procedure anew. Are there more effective ways to do the job? What would save time and money? Are all the steps necessary? Employees can embrace change and create a better job. This approach is energizing as they become not victims but agents of change and are an integral part of the process. It is as stimulating as having a new job—only better because they do not have to start over somewhere else.

Ann's job was repetitive. She worried her boss would find out. She quietly did her job and avoided discussion about her work. She was terrified the new boss would take a good look at all the jobs in the company and she would be out. To save herself she made an analysis of the work and discovered some related tasks that would be appropriate for her to handle. By combining a couple of functions she could drop her busy work and have a real job. She was eager to propose this to the new manager. Her ideas were considered and seen as constructive.

Jack wanted the plant to manufacture a new product. He brought up the subject to everyone who would listen. It got to be a joke. Now Jack had somebody new with whom he could discuss the plan. He carefully detailed the pros and cons, the possible extra expense, the projected profit, and how the product would fit in with what was presently manufactured. The new boss liked it, but was not ready to move on it until he was better acquainted with the operation. In the meantime he directed Jack to research further so he could have answers to specific questions. Jack felt encouraged and elated.

Steps to new directions:
1. Make sure present goals coincide with the new manager's goals.
2. Further the company's goals with every action.
3. Verify whether or not the work should continue as before or change to fit a new system.
4. Ask the boss for guidance if new directions are unknown or unclear.
5. Make suggestions that are good for the employees, the boss, and the company. Look for win-win opportunities.

6. Be part of the change process by reinventing the job.
7. Make the job a better job.

TACTIC # 7: BE SEEN, BE AVAILABLE, AND KEEP THE BOSS INFORMED

Robert made his presence known. He was loud and intrusive, but willing and able. The willing-and-able part helped him keep his job.

Some people have a knack for being seen at the right time and in the right place (Brothers, 1978). When the boss looks for someone with whom he or she can talk, they uncannily pick that night to work late and are available to be the boss's confidant. An important client breezes into the office without an appointment and they are there. How do they do this? Is it all luck? Not really. Can they put the technique into words? Probably not. Some people unconsciously tune into people in authority and know when to be where. They learned early in life to focus on the needs of those who are in higher authority because they needed to know when it was safe or when they could get approval. Most people have to learn the secret of availability. It is a secret that can now be told and can be learned. Study the boss to learn the boss's habits. When does the boss arrive for work, take breaks, catch up on work, go for lunch, make trips to the water cooler? When does the boss want to work uninterrupted and when does he or she wander the halls looking for conversation or an exchange of ideas?

Just being available is not enough. People who are seen hanging around do not make a positive impression. People who listen, have ideas, and volunteer to help are seen as responsive and responsible. Having a new boss is like having a new job. In a new job, employees go out of their way to look good and develop a good reputation. The same is appropriate when there is a new boss. Employees who know things that are helpful to new management make themselves valuable resources. If they know how to write grants, fix things, or know where everything is kept, they have something to offer.

The new boss did not know Robert's job. Robert did not ascribe to the idea that the boss would eventually notice him. He made himself available. He became friends with the boss's secretary. Robert had been with the company for a long time and knew who was who and what was where. When the secretary needed information he called Robert. Robert became a dependable resource for the boss's secretary. The new boss recognized this and called on Robert directly. This led to discussion, which led to an alliance that resulted in a close and comfortable working arrangement.

The boss wants to see employees working, coming in on time and not knocking off early. Employees know they are working, but bosses do not always know that. It is beneficial to the employees to know the boss's quirks and work with them. It is irritating to have a boss who has to always know the employees' whereabouts, or the status of the work. It is helpful to remember that the boss is that way because of his problem, not the employees' problems. Employees who help the new boss adjust to them, benefit from their efforts (Redford, 1978).

Lucy did some of her best work on the telephone. She was most comfortable and productive sitting in her bed while she made sales calls. Her ability was known. She did not hide her work methods. Her former boss had no problem as he knew she did what she was hired to do. The new boss only knew he never saw her around the office. This made him nervous and he began to distrust Lucy. He finally had a talk with her and insisted she work from the office like everyone else. If she took liberties, everyone would. Lucy had to work at her desk. Her productivity was good, but Lucy was not happy. She could not understand why the boss was so picky. When she realized it was the boss's problem and need, she did not take it personally and accepted the change.

Scott, on the other hand, fit right in with the boss's style. He loved to be seen. He wanted to be noticed and get feedback. He was happy to report regularly. The new boss, who liked to have his finger on everybody's pulse, worked well with Scott and saw him as a perfect employee.

Just because the boss earns the big bucks, it is not the boss's job to figure out what the employees are doing. It is up to the employees to let the boss know how they are contributing to the company's bottom line. If employees wait for the boss to acknowledge their work, they may wait too long and develop resentments because they are not consulted or end up left out of consideration for plum assignments because the boss reached an erroneous conclusion about the employee's job. Both employees and bosses are better off when the boss knows what the employee is doing. Let the boss know what is being done, keep up with the work, and do not miss deadlines ("Don't Hide," 1992). If the boss is not interested in hearing in person, a written memo explaining how the employee fits into the company's function is an excellent way to share this vital information. Employees want to include:

- The exact nature of the work, whether it is educational, informational, community oriented, customer service, production line work, supervision, clerical, research, technical, quality control, or several of these.
- References to the job description, describing how the work is done to meet the requirements.
- Who works on the same projects or directly with the employee.
- Who depends on the employee's work.
- All who need what the employee does in order to do their work.
- How many people give the employee work and how it fits in with production.

- Who receives work assignments from the employee and what kind of work is assigned.
- An explanation of how and when reports are made to the boss.
- Special assignments.
- Present projects, what they are, who assigned them, the status of each assignment, why they are assigned to the employee, and when they will be completed.
- The employee's special skills and experiences and how they are or can be used to further the interests of the company.
- Any miscellaneous information not covered previously.

Take plenty of time to make the list representative of the extent of the job. The new manager is unlikely to be aware of every employee's resume and job description. Explain certain functions in detail, such as taking care of complaints. Every aspect of the endeavor, including the people involved, the time needed, and the anticipated results, can be defined. A short example of a typical situation dramatizes the function. If the employees get the opportunity to spell out their responsibilities in person, they are urged to be organized and succinct.

Bosses do not like surprises of any kind, good or bad. The new boss is under scrutiny and wants to be prepared. If there are problems, report them and include possible solutions.

Lynn worked part-time. She was essential to the company because of her skill and her degree. When the new boss arrived she continued to do as she always had. The boss was busy and gave most of his attention to the cash flow during the early months of his employment. By the time he got around to Lynn, she had lost interest in impressing him. She surmised he knew what she did and gave him a few vague indications. The boss asked, "That doesn't take much time, does it?" The boss decided Lynn was overpaid and underutilized and wondered if she was necessary to the operation.

Timothy, who felt insecure, made a much better impression on the boss than did Lynn. He was prepared. He had his work detailed in written form and used this as a basis to explain his various responsibilities, why what he did was imperative to the company, and how he worked with other departments and coworkers. He asked about ongoing and special projects and suggested some ventures the boss might want to consider. He pointed out how he could and would be glad to take them on.

Some techniques for being seen, being visible, and keeping the boss informed are as follows:

1. Tune in to the boss's habits and needs.
2. Study the boss's routine and work habits.
3. Be useful.
4. Be seen working.
5. Keep a regular work schedule.
6. Explain any unusual work habits or unscheduled breaks.
7. Report whereabouts and accomplishments when away from the office.
8. Let the boss know how the work contributions coincide with the aims of the company.
9. Protect the boss from surprises. Keep the boss informed of foreseeable problems and make suggestions for solutions.
10. Bring the boss up-to-date on ongoing projects.

TACTIC # 8: UNDERSTAND THE JOB DESCRIPTION AND ENLARGE ON IT

When Bennett learned the company had been sold, the first thing he did was review his job description. He wanted to see if what he did was useful to the incoming managers.

The job description is a neglected and uninteresting item until someone makes it important. It is used to make sure employees are doing what they are hired to do, to keep them from doing what bosses do not want them to do, and to get rid of people by providing proof that they do not abide by the job description. New employers may have little interest in the job description or might determine an employee's ranking through use of the job description. When new management ascends, it is time to dust off the personnel manual in general and the job description is particular. It is the backbone of the employee's work position. It is the guide of what can and cannot be required of workers.

It is likely that the job description does not accurately describe what an employee does. Jobs, held over a period of time, evolve to meet the needs of the company and exploit each employee's talents. Employees will want their job descriptions to reflect what they really do and should revise their description accordingly so the new manager understands their contributions.

When the new boss is ready to look at individual jobs or the employee is assigned inappropriate or demeaning work, the time is right to discuss the job description. However, most job descriptions have clauses stating the employee will be assigned other job-related tasks, or the more general, other tasks as assigned, or that the job includes, but is not limited to, the responsibilities listed. This gives employers a great deal of leeway in what they can ask the employees to do. It also gives the employees latitude and the potential for enlarging their jobs and promoting their own position within the company. Employees who want to keep their jobs accept additional assignments. Experience in more areas makes employees more valuable (Schoenberg, 1978).

Nancy was one of the few employees carried over from the previous workforce. She had a new boss and practically all new coworkers. The new boss fired everyone who did not vow immediate allegiance, had consumer complaints against them, and did not seem to be performing an essential service. Nancy was left without her familiar communication and support system. No one was available to answer her telephone, type her letters, assist as needed, or locate her when she left the office. She spent an inordinate amount of time providing her own support services and checking with the office to see if she was needed. It became apparent that someone had to manage the office work. Nancy was asked to do it since she knew the system. To relieve the feeling of chaos and keep her job, she agreed officially to take on the added work. Then she read a help wanted advertisement in the newspaper that described her job. She was furious. She had knocked herself out to contribute and her boss was trying to replace her. She made herself wait until she calmed down. Then she saw her boss, confronted him with the job advertisement, explained her job description, and said she would do the additional work only if she had time after she did her defined job, and she expected to get paid for any overtime work. Since she was on a roll she told him there was a need for office staff and that was what he should advertise for. The boss heard her assertive statements, asked her to write out all she usually did and promised clerical back-up. Both kept their agreement.

Dennis's old boss retired. He had guided the company to the threshold of a new era of expansion before he left. The new boss was touted as the person who would help the company maintain stability as it grew. The growth, however, was so rapid that he had trouble hiring and training the ever-increasing number of employees. He needed help with new employee orientation and instruction for the short period of time it took to increase the workforce to its ultimate number. He asked the experienced employees to take new recruits under their wings and guide them until they could function independently. Dennis refused. He said it was not in his job description, he did not want to do it, and he was already too busy. He was not dissuaded from taking this stance when he was told that training new employees would result in relief from the increasing demands and that it would not be a permanent assignment. The company planned to hire a recruiter and training supervisor. Dennis did not relent. Dennis's boss was unfavorably impressed, but accepted his viewpoint as he needed to keep a person with Dennis's experience on the job. The employees who helped were rewarded with a dinner, special recognition, and a plaque. Dennis was not invited. He also did not get promoted to one of the supervisory positions that were created as the company continued to prosper and grow.

The message here is to heed the following advice:
1. Review the job description.
2. Determine its accuracy.
3. Discuss the job description with the new boss.
4. Allow leeway for "other duties as assigned."
5. Use the job description to avoid unwanted, unrelated work, or to take on wanted, related work.

TACTIC # 9: DO THE JOB

Mark, along with his coworkers, had no clue what new management would bring. He decided to coast until he found out. He neglected his work rather than make decisions and continue ongoing projects for fear he might do something the new boss might not want him to do. Mark thought he had made an intelligent decision. But what he did was appear indecisive, unmotivated, and irresponsible.

New management brings a time of distraction, dissension, and sometimes discouragement. It is hard to keep one's mind on one's job. Although employees feel they are working hard and are investing time and energy in the job, it is easy to slack off when there are new people and new procedures. The new ways are not as efficient because new moves take thought before they become comfortable and automatic. There are new people to meet. There is discussion among coworkers who want to catch up with the latest rumors about new management. No one wants to miss anything for fear they will miss out. It is hard to work as usual when work is not as usual. However, there is no change in the fact that all employees are responsible for their jobs and they have a commitment to the work (Amos, 1994) even if they have not made up their minds about their commitment to new management. When employees do not do their jobs they do hurt new management, but mainly they hurt themselves by damaging their work reputations. If one resents new management, it is hard to feel motivated. Motivation then has to come from within—one wants to do a good job because one is a good worker.

The regular outside reinforcers for a job well done are no longer available as the composition of the workforce has changed. Workers can reinforce themselves from within by reminding themselves why they want to keep the job. Employees can congratulate themselves for managing in the face of stressful change or pat themselves on the back for rising above the irritations of the situation.

The adjustment process is time limited because the new becomes the known after a fairly short period of time. The more accepting the attitude, the easier the transition. And if the stress does not let up because the new boss is happiest when surrounded by dissension and disruption, that too changes. Bosses change jobs. Employees can outlast them.

Mona was miserable. She felt she was in an endless dark tunnel. She felt the new boss undermined everything that made the agency a responsive and well-organized entity. The boss seemed determined to ruin the agency's reputation in the community and keep the staff stirred up by emphasizing petty problems. Feelings of insecurity increased as first one and then another staff member became the target in a campaign of harassment. Staff members were called down for minor infringements of agency policies and quit in anger and frustration. Mona liked her work but felt unable to do her job because she was always preoccupied with the latest outrage. She marveled at her friend Allen who saw his clients, kept his schedule, wrote grants that would benefit the agency, made speeches on behalf of the organization, and did not get bogged down in gripe sessions with his coworkers. She was irritated that he was not upset. It seemed disloyal to the rest of the staff. Mona asked him how he did it. Allen explained he knew everyone was having an awful time. He was not happy with the changes either, but he concentrated on doing his job as well as he could. He remarked that his experience in the armed forces prepared him for just such an event. He talked of his survival training and how it helped him concentrate on essentials and made him realize that it was important to do what had to be done in order to survive. The new boss lasted for two years. Allen lasted longer. While many of his coworkers quit in despair, Allen did not shirk his work. He kept his job, his boss did not. Neither did Mona. She thought it her responsibility to spend time in subversive activities against the administration rather than put the energy into her work. She burned out and had to move on.

When new people and new directives change the tenor of the operation, it is easy to blame circumstances for not doing one's job. Granted, it is hard when others do not perform according to expectations and former routine. This makes it difficult to concentrate on the work. It is easy to lose heart, give up, and think that individual work makes no difference. Nevertheless, the employee's job is to do his or her work with salvation from stress coming from his or her focus on the work. When they are more sensitive to what others are doing or not doing they are sabotaging their own work and security. Whether or not employees approve of each others' work methods is immaterial as coworkers do not have the authority to make each other change work habits and techniques or to fire their coworkers. All an employee can do is make sure he or she is doing his or her job as it should be done and trust that coworkers and the boss notice that they are doing a good job. Individual employees can set a standard for the rest of the staff. They teach by example while freeing themselves from worrying about the performance of the new workers and the new administration.

Employees who change jobs usually do so not because of the work but because of work stresses, differences with administration, and personnel problems. One way to keep from leaving in defeat is to concentrate on the job and forget about personnel concerns and the work performance of others.

When there is new management, it is the employee's job to match his or her work to the ideas and directions of the new boss, not vice versa. Try to follow directives and improve performance at the same time. See change as absorbing rather than disturbing. Employees who concentrate on their work and understand the new plan become excited and energized rather than befuddled and unwilling. Awareness of the changes and concentrating on how to make them work enables the worker to understand the "present situation more clearly" (Stephens, 1991: 26).

Even if the mandated proposals have been tried unsuccessfully in the past, the workers' responsibility is to try to make them work, knowing that the "new" plan is being tried in an altered environment, during a new era, and under different management. If problems arise, the boss can then be notified.

Harry was one of the few remaining employees who had a long relationship with the organization. Most of the others left immediately or soon after the new administration took over. As a result, the administrator hired new people eager to follow her direction. She charted a new course and did not consult Harry on the subject of the way the work was previously done. Harry was beside himself as he was sure his team members did not understand the priorities. Different features of the job were emphasized. These elements of the job were not his priorities, nor did he think they were the proper priorities. This gnawed at him and he spent so much time predicting calamitous results that he became too depressed to do his job. The new employees discharged their responsibilities with dispatch, but Harry lagged behind. When he awakened to the fact that work was progressing just fine, it was almost too late for him to start producing. However, he pulled himself together, became part of the effective team, and worked well with the group. He saw that different priorities did not change the quality of the product.

Jennifer was not to be outdone by the new employees. She wanted them to know she had experience, knowledge, and ability. Whatever they had done, she had done more of it. When they indicated they could perform some special service, she let them know she could too, but better. She put her effort into showing up the new employees the manager brought with her. As a result, she neglected her routine duties, fell behind, had to be confronted with her poor performance, and was put on probation. She felt picked on and continued to put more time into competing than into performing her assigned duties. She was unable to hold on to her job.

See the importance of the job and concentrate on doing it:

1. As long as the job continues, employees continue to have responsibility for it.
2. Employees can give themselves reassurance that they are doing a good job and feel satisfaction in their continued good work habits.
3. Develop an immunity to the irritation of change.
4. Recognize that an adjustment period is time-limited.
5. Know that change can be tolerated.
6. Keep up with the work even if the boss is a loser.
7. Do a good job to keep a good work reputation.
8. Tune in to what needs to be done rather than what others are or are not doing.
9. Model good work habits.
10. Keep an open mind about new procedures.
11. Adjust work to new standards and styles.
12. See change as improvement.
13. Cooperate rather than compete.

TACTIC # 10: USE MEMOS

Helen had many questions about her relationship with the company's new owners. They held meetings and gave the staff members a good deal of information, but Helen's anxiety made it difficult for her to understand what they were saying. Were personnel and work policies changing or remaining the same? Was her job going to change or go on as always? She needed information in writing.

In a state of flux, employees are torn between the old and the new in a myriad of ways. If old instructions were written, these feel the safest to use. If new management proposes new policies and procedures and there is nothing in writing, it can be uncomfortable. In many new companies structure is so fluid that there is no possibility of getting anything but the most general personnel policies in writing. And this is more and more the type of management that is emerging. To keep an organization flexible, ironclad rules are an abomination. Nevertheless, employees need to know what the new management is prepared to give them in the way of compensation, vacation, sick leave, and insurance. It is appropriate that these items are written. Also, special assignments can be put in writing. This is especially important if the employees fear they will be left out on the ledge if something goes wrong. They want to know that the company stands behind them and they want credit for any extraordinary effort they put forth. A memo of assignment or understanding in the employee's personal record is good to have if they are to be considered for other jobs in the company or if they want to add the experience to their resume.

If the employees do not get the essential information they want in writing, they can write a memo of understanding, stating that they want to be sure they are clear about the assignment, agreement, or directive. They can ask the boss to sign their memo to verify that they are in agreement, both comprehending the instructions in the same way. This is important when the assignment is out of the ordinary and when the employees fear they are going to be held solely responsible if there are repercussions. If the boss will not sign the memo, the staff member has every reason to wonder why. If this is the case, the employees are right to question how far they want to go on the basis of the verbal terms. There certainly is no general rule that fits all that could possibly go wrong. Employees can go ahead with the assignment if they are confident of the boss's integrity, they can appeal to a higher-up for approval and sanction if they are not so confident, or they can write a private memo, and file it among their private and project papers. If the later tack is taken, the employee should append follow-up documentation of all his or her and the boss's actions and directions.

Employees who want ongoing documentation of their work performance should save memos commending outstanding or extra work and make notes about activities that go beyond the call of duty. This paperwork comes in handy during performance reviews or when recent work is criticized. Over time, it is easy to forget past contributions, ignore superior performances, or take employees for granted. Even if such documentation is not needed for official purposes, it is good for the employees' self-esteem, particularly during times when the work is stressful and the future insecure.

Ron was delighted to learn he would get two days off for every 60 sales he made. The boss wanted to set new records and Ron wanted extra time away from work. He made the sales and took the time. Later, while scheduling his annual vacation, he saw the two days subtracted from his earned vacation time. He asked the boss to correct the mistake. His boss told him he did not mean he could have two days in addition to his vacation time. He meant that Ron would deserve time off if he produced in record numbers. Ron did not quit over this episode, but he never made another agreement with this boss without getting it in writing.

Rena was asked to delete certain files from the computer. She said she would be glad to do it, but could not without written orders. The orders never came.

Bosses, like everyone else, get distracted, misunderstand, misinterpret, and hear what they want to hear. They miss the point, think they are discussing something in the abstract instead of agreeing to an actual plan, or think the issue is related to something else altogether. The boss may have an entirely different frame of reference than the speaker, may not be feeling well, may have a hard time concentrating, or may habitually forget much of what is said (Bern, 1987). These are among the many reasons why it is wise to receive confirmation in memos.

For Your Information (FYI) memos are a good idea when the boss in interested in ongoing information about a project, when something new or unique occurs, or if there is information crucial to the company. If employees reach an outstanding point in their work or want to share information on a conference, verify progress on a work assignment, or make a request for time off or an expenditure, the memo is a great tool and a good protective measure.

Some bosses do not like memos, preferring to talk to employees. Of course, employees learn their bosses' preferences and inclinations and conform. This does not mean the employees should never write a memo. Memos are still appropriate to verify plans and confirm instructions. But they should be succinct and to the point. Too many words are irritating and unnecessary.

Keep memos where they can be retrieved to clarify understanding and even to save the day when a boss needs help knowing when and why something was done.

Elizabeth's boss did not want anything in writing. She thought something in writing would and could be held against her. Elizabeth, on the other hand, wanted everything in writing. When she found a good way to do something she wanted to pass the word. It was not necessary, she thought, for everyone to learn everything for themselves. Conveying the information verbally did not work as coworkers forgot and then did not have anything to refer to. Elizabeth thought too much knowledge was lost, but she did not want to go against her new boss. She complied, but kept a memo file, sharing copies with coworkers if they asked. One day the boss asked Elizabeth about something she had previously mentioned and Elizabeth pulled out the pertinent memo. Not long after the boss asked Elizabeth to share her FYI memos with her.

Donald was a dynamic person with a great deal of energy. He had many ideas and put them into practice. No one questioned his dedication or ability, but the new boss could not keep up with him and was constantly quizzing Donald about his work, asking other employees if they had seen Donald, and nervously requesting Donald to check in with him. Donald felt insulted that the new boss did not trust him. But he did not want to lose his job and he wanted to help the boss. He started writing the boss FYI memos letting the boss know what he was doing and where to reach him. He also outlined details of plans for future work, and if they seemed risky, asked the boss to approve or disapprove of them. They developed a communication method that put the boss at ease and gave Donald the freedom he needed.

A memo a day keeps the boss at bay. Some suggestions:
1. Follow up a verbal report with a memo to clarify and verify and to make sure the boss heard what was said.
2. Write out the boss's instructions and verify them with him or her.
3. Keep the boss posted on absences, discoveries, and work in progress.
4. Save memos for backup and reference.
5. Write memos to share knowledge.
6. Request documentation of special assignments for the personnel file.

7. Write memos and document progress about work assignments that aren't in writing and keep them in a private file.

8. Get written verification of unusual personnel agreements.

CHAPTER THREE REVIEW

1. Do personal work goals coincide with the company's goals?
2. Is there visibility and ability to help when the boss needs it?
3. Is the job description available and the contents known?
4. Have work plans been checked out with the new boss?
5. Is work kept up-to-date so the reputation as a good worker is maintained?
6. Is new management seen as an opportunity to redefine the job?
7. Is every effort being made to follow the new standard operating procedure?
8. Are memos used to verify understanding of assignments, agreements, and directives?
9. Are verbal reports confirmed with written reports?
10. Are memos short and to the point?
11. Are memos saved for followup and backup?

CHAPTER 4

HAVE FUN

Ira saw work as a serious matter. He put all his thoughts and time into this priority. He became grim because the job problems drained his attention and energy. He was not enjoying life and no one was enjoying his companionship. It was time to reevaluate his approach.

A major portion of life is spent in the workplace. Should people be unhappy during this big chunk of time? True, a job is a serious matter, but workers are not obligated to make work one dour day after another. That is simply too much to ask, no matter how desperately a person wants to keep the job. Misery is better left to martyr types.

TACTIC # 11: GIVE PEP TALKS, LOOK FOR POSITIVES, AND REMEMBER WHY THE JOB IS IMPORTANT

Marjorie was negative. Her mind was busy with work problems. Everything was difficult and wrong. She did not see her employment problems as challenges and opportunities. The self-talk she engaged in was doing her harm. She needed to give herself some pep talks.

Pep talks are a self-talk technique in which the workers emphasize their good qualities and focus on the facts of the situation. Employees who use pep talks stick with the positive and tell themselves that the work is going all right, they have done nothing wrong, are causing no problems, are not responsible for everything that happens, and are not alone in their concerns. Pep talks help people hold their fire, get more facts, stay out of trouble, feel in control, and remain in touch with reality.

Employees fear that if they talk themselves into positive moods and actions and develop self-confidence in the face of work changes they will miss some ominous menace and, consequently, end up exposed to a job danger they could have foreseen. In fact, the opposite is true. A positive outlook offers a more relaxed view which makes people better able to objectively analyze what is actually going on. A negative frame of reference gives employees a mindset that interprets everything from a pessimistic premise. Everything that new management does is seen as disastrous and aimed at getting rid of the employees. All that anyone says or does means something more than is meant, and in the end is thought to be directed at them as disapproval. Not only is this fatalistic approach torturous, it is ruinous. Sad sacks do not do well at home or at work. People avoid, criticize, and lose patience with them. Simply put, operating from the basis of hopelessness leads to bad decisions. Positive pep talks help to thwart ill-founded conclusions and impulsive, poorly thought out actions.

Pep talks help employees get more facts before making a decision (Watson, 1991). Employees problem solve rather than panic. They check out rumors and quiet their concerns while they gather more information. They keep themselves steady and on course.

Susan knew "they" were after her when her medical insurance claim came back saying her policy had been terminated. She saw this as a sure sign the new manager was trying to get rid of her, did not care enough about her work to keep her informed, or was so incompetent or insensitive that this action was a foreshadowing of future abominations. Since the notice came to her home via mail on a Friday, she could not confront anyone regarding the problem until Monday. She had two full days to work herself into a frenzy. She did not use the time that way, however. She instead gave herself a pep talk during which she thought of other possibilities for what had happened. Perhaps the insurance company made a mistake. Maybe the bookkeeper erred. In the meantime she checked her contract and reassured herself that the company was responsible for paying her insurance. With this fact in mind she stopped stewing and enjoyed her weekend.

Pep talks and positive thinking can get human beings through gloomy times. Positive thinking takes effort because people tend to be programmed with negatives. This is how many children become socialized. They are trained by "don't" and "no" commands. Their natural energy, curiosity, and exuberance are curtailed to make them acceptable in public places and around people. So negative job information heaped on negative training can lead to negative overload. Overwhelmed employees get stuck in the gloom and doom of the negative unless they make an effort to see the positive. The sooner employees get to work on improving their viewpoint, the sooner they start feeling good (Dyer, 1978). The benefits of positive thinking are:

1. There are more cheerful feelings.
2. The feelings of doom fade.
3. People feel healthier.
4. Employees appear to be more confident and capable.
5. Positive people are liked.
6. Friends and relatives do not get overloaded with the employee's negative attitudes.
7. Time is not wasted on worrying about things that may never happen.
8. Employees are more cooperative and enthusiastic. This is appreciated.

9. People who are positive during stressful times are admired for their ability to handle pressure situations.
10. It is more fun.

Al's modus operandi was to protect himself from disappointment, often at all costs. He did this by always expecting the worst and reading negatives into every thought, word, and deed. He had plenty of practice and was good at it. So when the CEO was replaced he handled it by doing what he normally did. He worried. He predicted disaster. He was a pain to himself and others. So what happened? The new CEO did some things very well, did some things that were not popular with the staff, and avoided Al because of his obvious negative attitude. One of the items on the new manager's agenda was the appointment of an assistant. Because of his experience and expertise, Al was considered for the position. Because of his attitude and comportment, he was not selected.

It is hard to stay positive in the face of unwelcomed changes. Nevertheless, everything does not change. It is positive to think about the reasons for keeping the job. If those positive reasons remain the same, employees can remind themselves of their original decision and enumerate the important elements that were the basis for their determination to struggle and survive new management. Getting past what is not liked and remembering what is liked is working with the positive. When employees decide to stay, it does them little good if they stay and act churlish. If they carry off their decision to stay with grace and good humor they are likely to do well. Employees who have reasons for staying want to keep these reasons in mind when the following occurs:

- They are criticized.
- Old management is criticized.
- Procedures and policies are changed.
- Work schedules are revised.
- Benefits are revised.

- Traditions are ignored.
- Established work habits are questioned.
- New employees get credit for work techniques established workers have been using.
- New employees are not doing good work.
- Changes occur without notice.
- There is a desire to act on angry feelings.

Leroy walked out when his friend was fired. Friendship and loyalty aside, he felt this coworker was essential to the organization. His protests to new management were heard, but the decision was not overturned. Though Leroy believed he was doing the right thing, his actions did not help his friend, and they certainly did not help him. Think of it: He was without a job. What did his own unemployment solve? He acted without thinking about his reasons for wanting to stay on the job, or about what was best for him and his family.

Mary was switched from customer service to accounting. She was a "people person," not a numbers cruncher. She was irate. However, she reminded herself of her reasons for wanting her job and did the best she could in her new position. She kept her job and continued to be involved with people because her accounting job included helping middle management supervisors with the budget process. Since she remembered why she wanted to stay employed, she did not spend time indulging in aggravation about the change. She put her energy into doing a good job in her new decision. She kept an open mind and found she liked her new position. Since she hob-knobbed with the supervisors, she was in an excellent slot for getting to know the people who could help her get ahead. What had seemed the worst possible situation turned out to be advantageous for Mary.

Some ways to maintain a positive attitude are as follows:

1. See positives in the change.
2. Take time to evaluate and get more facts.

3. Problem solve.

4. Give reassuring self-talk.

5. Have positive thoughts ready to replace negative thoughts.

6. Review reasons for staying with the job.

7. Let go of irritations that do not influence the decision to stay.

8. Be content with the decision to stay.

TACTIC # 12: HAVE FUN AT HOME AND WORK

Estelle kept a fixed demarcation between business and pleasure. She exercised her belief to such an extent that she did not discuss work at home or home at work. No one knew Estelle as a multi-faceted person. This strict separation of these aspects of her life kept her focused, but also made her boring. Her family wondered what her work was like and her coworkers wondered if she had a life outside of work.

If the job was fun BC (Before Consolidation), it can be fun AD (After Downsizing). Granted, being gobbled up by another company and the subsequent fear of being a victim of meaner and leaner management is not fun. Nevertheless, solemnity will not guarantee the job, it will just make it more tedious. All employees can do is all they can do. It is easy for someone not involved in the insecurity and struggle of new management to say that a bad time does not need to be made worse by bad feelings, but it is nevertheless the truth. Focusing on what is funny and fun assists in changing one's attitude and outlook and gives immediate relief from stress and tension.

If what employees liked about the job BC continues, there is no reason not to enjoy that part of the job. If old friends are still on the job, appreciate their company. If everybody is new, find pleasure in getting to know them.

When employees are overwhelmed with worry and negative emotions it usually shows. They can get out of this rut by acting happy. This is not being phony, this is self-improvement. It works because mood catches up with behavior and the feelings improve. Coworkers respond to a cheerful mood and give positive feedback. This, in turn, promotes good feelings that become the real thing.

Concentrating on the pleasant aspects of the job instead of the worries changes how people look at things. People can choose. They can notice pleasure or they can notice pain. By choosing pleasure they help themselves weather the bad times without bad feelings. Worrying does not prevent problems. Happiness doesn't change what happens either, but it minimizes suffering.

In any job, there are usually some activities employees look forward to doing each day, even if it is taking a break and going for lunch. If they concentrate on those activities there is always something pleasant to anticipate. It is better to fixate on something cheery and feel good than it is to focus on everything that is and can go wrong and feel miserable.

Joking and relating humorous anecdotes brightens the day, the workplace, and the employees' moods (Rubin, 1969). Telling family and friends about the funny things that happened at work also makes the employees more pleasant in the non-work area. Long-suffering relatives and neighbors can only take so much bad news and so many morbid forecasts, no matter how much they like the person. A word of caution: humor can be mean and spiteful. Seeing humor in the discomfort of others, or embarrassing the boss or coworkers, is not funny to them and will backfire. If employees can laugh at themselves, others are delighted to join in the hilarity. Humor helps employees transcend mistakes and humiliation.

A positive attitude is the successful result of looking for entertaining events both at work and at home. If work is tense there is every reason to have fun at home. Trouble in the workplace often spills over into worrying and tension at home. This makes a mess of the worker's entire life. Make work, and life after work, as pleasant as it can possibly be. Hang around cheerful people, make plans to do fun things, work at being good company, find entertainment that is relaxing and spawns chuckles, whether it be a funny movie, a TV sit-com, or a book. Fun and relaxation do not mean that everything has to be a riot. Hobbies, sports, shopping, telephone contacts, gardening, or any healthy diversion is engrossing and good for a downcast mood. The more beleaguered employees feel, the more they need to make the extra effort to enjoy their off-work hours.

If employees take good care of their moods, their good spirits enliven the workplace and their coworkers' days. Jokes and anecdotes are enlivening and so is thoughtfulness. People's lives go on even through stressful times. They still have birthdays, job anniversaries, and holidays to celebrate. Congratulating and complimenting coworkers at special times and observing special events boosts morale and builds support. Look for reasons for gaiety, such as getting to the bottom of the in-box, leaving work on time, or getting through another month, week, or day. The new boss might also catch the spirit and see the need for levity and caring in the workplace.

Henry was a nice guy. He could not be anything else. He ascribed to the model that NICE GUYS FINISH FIRST, even though he sometimes felt like a wimp. He revised his secret wimp image when he read that many of the successful people who run large companies are nice guys and front runners (Brophy, 1988). His ability to be nice became a cherished asset rather than a perceived fault, and this change enabled him to help his coworkers with confidence.

Ivan was not an effervescent, outgoing person. He did not think of himself as a leader. But he was determined to avoid getting pulled down emotionally by his dispirited coworkers. His approach was to listen and extract something positive from what they said. It helped them look at the situation from a more favorable point of view. Sometimes his determination to see everything as happening for the best was so farfetched it was laughable. But it kept Ivan cheerful. His coworkers looked forward to running every new directive or rumor past him to see if he could make it sound terrific without stretching credibility. Ivan maintained an upbeat mood and helped his coworkers elevate their moods too.

Harold loved to eat. He also loved to bake and was good at it. Changes in leadership did not deter him from bringing in the goodies he enjoyed sharing with his coworkers. He used any excuse as a reason for providing office workers with something good to eat. It was Monday. It was Friday. It was the middle of the work week. It was a birthday, a holiday, or just time to celebrate. Food did not cure the discontent, but was a nice distraction and good for morale.

Steps to having fun at home and at work include the following:

1. Enjoy what was always enjoyed at work and home.
2. Put on a happy face.
3. Concentrate on the pleasant.
4. Act with good humor.
5. Take a joke graciously.
6. See the humor in a situation.
7. Search for the positive.
8. Tell jokes and amusing anecdotes.
9. Be friendly.
10. Find reasons for celebrations, commendations, and compliments.
11. Entertain friends and family members with humorous anecdotes.
12. Schedule fun activities with cheerful people.

TACTIC # 13: FIND SUPPORT

Sam was new to the area and only a few months on the job when new management took over. His problem was that he felt isolated and alone. He had to find someone who could be a friend or he would go crazy. He did not think he could manage the tension by himself.

Employees who feel alone and without support during times of change experience feelings of loss and develop symptoms of stress. As we have seen, stress symptoms affect employees physically, emotionally, and behaviorally. People do not have to go through loss and stress all by themselves (Hyatt & Gottlief, 1987). Nor is it advised. Aloneness magnifies problems because there is no feedback, no objectivity, and a resultant feeling that no one cares.

Talking with trusted people is a handy stress reliever, but it is not advised that one talk to people indiscriminately (Rogers, 1973). As much as employees want to complain or share concerns, it is not wise to talk off the top of the head or be indiscreet. There are reasons for this.

1. Employees do not want new managers to think they are disgruntled, as disgruntled workers are not considered reliable. Impulsive and negative remarks are best discussed away from the workplace with a trusted confidant. If suggestions and criticisms are deemed appropriate for the new boss to hear, they can be given formally, in person, and during a scheduled appointment. Even then, new bosses do not want to hear complaints and if problems are reported they like to hear suggestions for solutions too. Employees who appear to have too many unanswerable problems are not trusted to do a good job.

2. Clamorous conversations with coworkers are seen as rabble-rousing. Employers want no part of people who incite others to act in opposition to new management.

3. Employees want to make favorable impressions on employers or others who write letters of recommendation. Workers want positive recommendations that do not include information indicating they cannot handle change or stress or that they are troublemakers.

4. Individuals who work in similar businesses like to hear rumors about their competitors' troubles. If they ask for

confirmation, only unwise employees take that as an opportunity to unburden themselves. Employees can acknowledge there are a few problems that are being addressed. If more distressing detail is shared, the curious rival sees the complainers as people who cannot work with a new boss, accept change, or handle stress. Someday they may want to work for their competitors and do not want their present distress to be held against them at that time.

5. Even if the employees are right about what is wrong, the complaints leave others with serious doubt about their stability. Grumbling makes employees sound anxious and disagreeable.

6. People who care about the employees, such as friends, relatives, neighbors, and coworkers are generally sympathetic, but soon find grouchiness tiresome and irritating. They get bored with the negativity.

7. Employees never know how coworkers will use the information they are given. For example, coworkers may report another worker's discontent to the new manager to promote their own self-interests. Fair-weather friends may use the employee's misfortune to make themselves feel superior.

8. Once words are spoken and heard they cannot be taken back. Apologies, explanations, and denials may be in order, but they do not erase what was said and what was heard.

9. Once grumbling is heard it becomes part of the image the employee projects to the supervisor, the coworker, or the new manager. When employees make an adjustment to the changed work environment, they cannot shake their image. It is part of them.

10. Emotional ultimatums over changes, such as, "I do not approve of this and I won't do it," put employees in an untenable position. They may have to do that which they do not care to do. They may, upon reflection, want to do it. During fluid job situations it is better to be wishy-washy than to live on the edge and take an unpopular and unfounded stand against

a policy, procedure, or work assignment. None may be so controversial or disagreeable that it is worth losing the job over.

11. Grumbling that deteriorates to personal attacks is especially unappealing to new management. It is unimportant if the new administrator's preferences do not coincide with the worker's or his or her taste is considered tacky. This has nothing to do with anyone's job qualifications and can only be considered sour grapes by anybody who overhears the gripes.

12. Coworkers who want to be happy with their jobs are happier if the discontented do not annoy them with their grousing (Coffin, 1975). They have enough problems and do not want to be alarmed by additional concerns.

Some people have problems finding and accepting support because they are stoics who think they should stiff-upper-lip-it through travail, or their personalities are such that they have a hard time talking to people about anything personal, much more so something so problematic as job fears. Some employees find themselves alone because of transfers to a new plant in an unfamiliar city or they do not know anyone they can trust with their worries.

It is not wrong for people to want to handle their own problems, to be cautious when picking confidants, and to feel support is not available when in a strange city with people they don't know. Nevertheless, there comes a time when it is healthier to share concerns. This is the case when job uncertainty is foremost in the employee's mind.

Finding a trustworthy person who listens, keeps confidences, is loyal, close-mouthed, available, and has the patience to hear repeated tales of unhappiness and hurt, is not a piece of cake. Possibilities include friends who can absorb the stress without having to discuss the matter with others, a person who lives in another area and does not know any of the participants, or a coworker who also needs a confidant. A coworker, if totally trusted, is a great confidant because the fellow employee has similar concerns and can discuss the work problem interminably without getting tired of endless analysis and repetition.

When people feel compelled to unload emotionally and do not have anyone close at hand to trust, they sometimes do the next best thing. Troubled people talk to seat mates on buses and airplanes, they seek out psychotherapists, they call crisis lines, or they respond at length when someone innocently asks them how the job is going. This is support, obtained when it is needed from any available resource. In such cases, workers have support from someone who is not involved in their problems and can listen objectively without anxiety and personal pain.

Employees can and do give themselves support through pep talks, positive self-talk, and remembering why they want to stay on the job. They can also use any known or newly learned stress reduction technique to ease them through the bad times. "Support" means different things to different people. Support can also include the following:

1. *Sharing activities.* Not everyone finds talking supportive. For some, mutually enjoyable activities are supportive.

2. *Learning.* Support can come in the form of classes or seminars on self-awareness, financial planning, communication, or job skills, for example.

3. *Being needed.* Feeling important to family, friends, and neighbors may be support for people who gain satisfaction from helping others. Volunteering and helping other people with problems can be very supportive because of the grateful feedback volunteers receive as a by-product of their good works.

4. *Keeping busy.* People who are happy when they are productive can keep themselves feeling good with projects and responsibilities. They feel worry-free when they are actively engaged and are accomplishing something.

5. *Getting reassurance.* Sometimes employees get their best support from checking with the boss and receiving assurance that they are doing well. Reassurance from coworkers

helps too, but does not carry the same authority as a good word from the boss.

William was transferred to another plant in another state because the plant he worked in closed down. He did not like it, but his financial security depended on making the move. His wife and children stayed in their home town to sell the house and get the children through the school year. William felt very alone and bereft of support. He talked with his family frequently, but did not want to worry them. So he established his own support group by finding other recently transferred workers. They felt they were in this together and enjoyed mutual activities and friendships.

Kristy had problems with new management and trouble talking to people because she was shy. She was embarrassed speaking up and could not think of the right words to say when opportunity presented itself. She got support through buying self-help books and taking a class on assertiveness at the community college. She felt better because she put her energy into self-improvement

Pamela tried to get along. She would rather do what she was asked than argue against it. However, her new boss seemed not to have read her job description and asked her to do jobs she considered beyond her scope or degrading. As this bothered her more and more, she became less and less cooperative. She did not do the job well, "forgot" to do it, or accepted the assignment in poor grace, showing her unhappiness in her agitated body movements, her frowning face, and her snappish tone of voice. She needed support, but her family was sick of her complaining and she did not trust anyone at work. She went to see a psychotherapist. It only took a few visits for her to clearly comprehend that what she was doing was not helpful to her and would not help her keep her job.

Clark was so upset he talked indiscriminately to anyone who would listen. This included his children, his bowling league teammates, anybody in the office break room, any church member who greeted him on Sunday morning, as well as friends and neighbors. People greeted him coolly and kept walking, avoided taking coffee breaks at the time he usually did, and made him as isolated as he felt. Incredibly none of this got back to his new boss. He kept his job and eventually settled down and resumed his normal pattern of behavior.

Find support this way:

1. Talk with others about problems.
2. Use positive self-talk for self support.
3. Talk with a psychotherapist.
4. Accompany a friend to mutually pleasurable activities.
5. Learn something new.
6. Give help to others and feel satisfaction in their gratitude.
7. Stay occupied and productive.
8. Get reassurance from the boss if there are doubts about the work.
9. Be discriminating about what is said to whom.
10. Say nothing rather than complain to someone who will use the words against you.
11. Stop boring people with continual complaining.
12. Talk to people who can keep confidences, are readily available, loyal, and have no need to fix things or give advice.
13. Aim for objectivity rather than fault finding.
14. Evaluate the job, not the person.

CHAPTER FOUR REVIEW

1. Are friends and relatives an important part of the employee's life?
2. Are enjoyable activities pursued?
3. Is concentration on what is going right?
4. Is humor noticed and enjoyed?
5. Is time spent with cheerful people?
6. Are coworkers congratulated and commended and are special events celebrated?
7. Are positives looked for and found?
8. Do employees know they can cope?
9. Are employees reminding themselves why they want to keep their jobs?
10. Are trusted people, who can be confidants, identified?
11. Is the employees' support system made up of themselves, other people, activities, coworkers, and projects?

CHAPTER 5

KEEP THE GOAL IN MIND

Weldon's associations were about to get him into trouble. He was actively involved with a group of coworkers who were circulating a petition to have their boss fired. His friends wanted him to sign and he agreed with their objective. He did not stop to think what would happen to him should their petition fail.

TACTIC # 14: AVOID ACTIVE PROTESTS

Roy put a notice on the bulletin board inviting all employees to a meeting to discuss the new policies. This alerted management and made them nervous. Roy's boss took it as subversion. If Roy wanted to scare the boss, he succeeded. But he did not do himself any good.

Change stirs up anti-change forces (Slavin, 1978). Dissenters have a seductive platform because they hold out the promise of success while offering hope for the possibility of returning to the status quo or preventing a takeover. They are enthusiastic and work to drum up support from the workforce. But in the end, no matter how worthwhile their project may be, it is doomed to failure. Employees are more preoccupied with keeping their jobs than in fighting change. Some secretly urge the conspirators to success, but continue to apply themselves to the jobs they are hired to do. There is little chance of an employee force winning over new management that is hired for a particular purpose and has the support of the board of directors.

The higher echelon will probably agree to talk to the agitators, but only in the hope that having their say will quiet them or they will be able to persuade these employees to stop their campaign. If the group can gather enough support, money, and evidence, they could manage to present their case in court. All this takes time, energy, and is emotionally draining. Change occurs no matter what staff members do. They are taking a perilous detour that stirs negative, but exhilarating emotions, and keeps them bitter and angry. Anyone who is involved with them is identified with the group. If employees join in the protest they are labeled "protesters." There is no way out except to say no and remember why the job is necessary to continued well-being.

Bob did not like the new policies. He was loyal to his old boss, whom he thought was treated shabbily. He wanted the board to know what was really happening in the company. He was sure they would revise their plan when they truly understood. He fully expected the board members to hear him out, see the folly of their ways, and return everything to the way it was. He organized his protest and enlisted a group of dissatisfied employees to accompany him to the board meeting. To his dismay, the new boss was present. The board members politely heard the presentation, thanked them for coming, and gave the new executive their vote of confidence. The employees were dumbfounded. Many recognized their defeat, settled down and got back to work, or found other jobs. A core group continued to work for a return to the status quo by talking with individual board members, writing letters to the editor of the newspaper, and passionately grumbling to any who would listen. They met regularly to plan strategy. Bob's bitterness increased as the effects of their efforts decreased. His time and energy was invested in a cause that gave him nothing in return.

Lauren was a good friend of the boss who was forced out. She was distressed for her friend and for the future of the company. Her distress continued as various employees, also her friends, were summarily relieved of their duties. She hated the entire process, but believed in the company, believed she performed valuable work, and did not want to leave. She remained sympathetic, but made no open protests. She made it clear that her plan was to stay employed. Her friends were disappointed in her. Some had nothing more to do with her. Others continued in the friendship, but they were more distant. She was sad for their misery, but was glad to remain in a job she liked. She was confident the company reorganization would work, and that she would feel the same zest for the work as she had in the past.

To keep from getting involved in active protests consider these suggestions:

1. Recognize that subversives do not help the employees and may hurt them.
2. Accept the fact that a decision against participation in a revolt draws disfavor from activist coworkers.
3. Listen to the protests, but do not act on them.
4. Use time and energy to do the job well.
5. Stand firm.

TACTIC #15: AVOID COMPLACENCY

George felt secure. He knew everything would work out fine. He did not want to pander to new management. He shunned office politics and saw no need to cater to the new boss. George was about to learn that politics can be more important than skills (Kennedy, 1980).

Employees who have had experience with change and learned they could live through it approach change differently than those who have never had the experience. The latter see change as the destruction of their work environment, their livelihood, and, ultimately, themselves. Employees who have been with the company for many years and always received good performance evaluations, have every right to feel well qualified. If they got along well with former executive officers, made contributions such as writing the policies and procedures for the department, and kept the company out of trouble during difficult times, they may well fell they can stand on their own records and not feel threatened by new management.

Employees who realize what they have to offer and recognize their successes have reason not to be nervous about new management. They feel confident and secure in their ability and accomplishments. That is not the same as complacency.

Complacency denotes self-satisfaction, which is not bad, but goes wrong when employees get stuck on self-satisfaction and make no effort to sell themselves or properly present what they can do, and yet expect new management to accommodate them, rather than vice versa.

Employees who are praised for their contributions and rewarded with promotions and salary increases tend to become complacent. When life is easy, friendly, and keeps getting better, it is understandable that they expect their careers to continue that way. This is a terrific feeling. They do not have a clue that any of this will change.

Everyone's complacency may be shaken by a new administration. The new boss does not take a good record for granted. Recognition and reward are not automatic in all circumstances. For this reason, it is important that employees let the new administrator know their job skills. The new boss does know, through study or reputation, that any one employee is competent and trustworthy. This is no time for employees to take their positions for granted.

This is the time to greet the new manager and offer information. Employees know how they can contribute, what they are doing, and where they need help. A new boss wants to have this information. Employees who offer help and information appear cooperative and confidant. Employees who do not reach out at this time come off as sullen and uncaring.

Complacent employees who are arrogant about their abilities and place in the organization are noticed not for their competence but for what appears to be their bad manners. Complacent employees who think they can compete on the basis of their reputation find this does not work with management types who are more interested in results than renown.

Michael was a top producer. Because of his reputation, he had many job offers. He did not accept them because he wanted to stay in the same place and benefit from the retirement plan he had invested so much time in. He enjoyed his work and saw no reason to change jobs. He was amply rewarded with pay and high regard from his employers and coworkers. He was secure and complacent. When the company was sold, Michael kept to his work with full confidence he would have no problems with new management. Everybody, he thought, knew he was good—look at all the job offers he'd turned down! This, however, was not simply a new chapter, it was a new book altogether. The new people did not look at his work record. They looked at his salary record and noted that he was about to cash in on his lucrative retirement plan. Michael showed little interest in them, which made them suspicious, thinking he might be planning to coast until he could draw on his benefits. They had serious concern, but did not discuss it with Michael, nor did he do anything to reassure their fears. But his work record and popularity were not enough, and he was let go. Both Michael and the new administration lost out.

Brenda had every reason to feel good about herself. She was working in a prestigious law firm and expected to be made a partner within a year. Although her mentor recently retired she was not worried because she knew she did good work and was admired for her creativity and diligence. Another excellent attorney was also up for a partnership. One day this attorney did something Brenda did not like. Without exploring why it happened, Brenda verbally attacked her. Her success had gone to her head. She felt she could say what she wanted because she was a star performer. When this attorney made partner before Brenda, she made sure Brenda's success stood for little in the firm. Brenda did not get a partnership. In fact, her life at work was so miserable she finally quit and went to work elsewhere.

The following are steps to counteract complacency:

1. Give the new boss information on experience and ability.
2. Volunteer information and skills.
3. Be ready to change with the needs of the company.
4. Demonstrate ability to function as a team player.

TACTIC # 16: AVOID CLIQUES

Garland was a cheerful worker, not because he liked his work, but because he loved the workplace and his group of friends there. He looked forward to exchanging jokes, pleasantries, and gossip. He was not particularly loyal to the company, but he was loyal to his friends.

An employee's best friends may be the ones most damaged by new management. This is, at best, difficult, and, at worst, intolerable. But it really is just a symptom of new management. Garland and his friends were dispatched to different departments so they no longer worked together. Some were given jobs they felt were below their abilities. They were more than upset, they were incensed.

The disruption of a cherished work group often results in sorrow and stress. But cliquish and contentious behavior does not serve any purpose for employees who want to keep their jobs. Employees united against the boss are not acceptable to new management. Such actions do not help workers keep their jobs. It is not suggested that workers ignore their friends, but employees need not devote themselves to one group. It is not disloyal to be friendly to many people.

If employees belong to a clique-that is, a small exclusive group of people-they are identified with it. Since it is exclusive, it does not expand to include others. This isolates members of the clique from other viewpoints and ideas. It limits opportunities. Belonging to a clique is dangerous because cliques have a character. All members of the clique are characterized by what the clique is known to represent. If members do not share all the attitudes and beliefs of other clique members, it makes no difference. They are seen as a typical clique member and risk destroying their chances for continuing their jobs in good standing with the new administration (Patton & Giffin, 1981).

It is painful to break with a clique when those coworkers are comfortable constants in the changing job scene. However, if the clique puts the employee's job in jeopardy, and the priority is the job, the choice is made. When this is the case, the rest of the group can profit from the wisdom of the person who wants to keep the job. They too may want to be seen as independent from any group that influences their thoughts and actions in a way that is perceived as acting against new management.

In Paul's eyes, new management made too many changes that were too disruptive. Whenever anything new was proposed, Paul met with a coterie of coworkers who did not like what was happening. They were often found behind closed doors inflaming each other with their thoughts. They hung together, needing each other for support. The more they isolated themselves from the rest of the workers, the more they felt like outcasts, and the more they leaned on each other. When further layoffs were planned, management aimed to get rid of the group members who would not integrate, fought every management suggestion, and were uncooperative.

Frances also opposed change. Some of her friends had their jobs eliminated. She was sad and in emotional pain. She wanted to keep her job, but did not want the new administration to succeed. However, since so many of her pals no longer worked in the company she had to make new friends or be alone. Since she was not a loner she got acquainted with other workers who continued their employment and with the new employees who replaced the workers who left. She was involved with a group of people who wanted the company to succeed. In conversation she heard positive ideas and hopes that helped her deal with her fears and worries. She had no personal or professional problems with keeping her job.

Instead of being cliquish consider the following:
1. Be friendly with many people.
2. Stay independent from cliques.
3. Talk to numerous people to get various ideas and opinions.

TACTIC # 17: SIDESTEP THE RUMOR MILL

Agnes lived for gossip. With the job site rife with rumor and innuendo she was nestled in her realm. Facts were dull. Agnes thrived on gossip because her joy was getting information and passing it on. Since what the gossip implied never upset her it never occurred to her that she was upsetting others with her colorful commentary.

Gossip is interesting, but with new management, only facts are really helpful. Employees want to know about developments that affect them. With knowledge, they can prepare themselves for what comes next. Employees look for clues about their future anywhere they can find them (Woodward & Buchholz, 1987). It is in changing times that innocent statements and actions of people who seem to know something take on momentous meaning. The appearance of a stranger or an unscheduled staff meeting is analyzed and discussed. Employees who appear to have inside information get attention and respect. In such a situation it is easy to poison the atmosphere with false rumors, anxious predictions, and angry accusations. When upset workers are in a state of unrest, it takes little to exacerbate the situation.

Employees do not help themselves or each other by passing on rumors and ominous forecasts. Employees who want to help themselves and their coworkers trace the rumors to their origin and work to get the facts. Employees who have legitimate information may not be as exciting as the ones who have lots of titillating gossip, but they are reassuring. They know more and speculate less.

Digging for facts may be difficult, or as simple as asking someone who has official access to information. If facts can be obtained and disseminated, they quell employee uneasiness better than can anything else. The employee who manage to become the sanctioned spokesperson for the harbingers of change gains respect from the staff members who are clambering for information and from managers who want the employees to assist in the changeover. The employees who get the facts that stop the rumors cannot be too careful about the information passed on to the staff. The spokespersons do not want to be party to half-truths designed to tranquilize the workforce, nor seen as mouth-pieces for management. Smart managers do not withhold the truth and smart employees do not pass on misinformation.

Fred knew of another job in his field. His qualifications made him a front-runner for the position. He did not want to leave the company, but was afraid new management would withhold the benefits he wanted and needed. He wanted to know what was happening to the health benefits and asked his coworkers. He heard rumors that the medical benefit package would be abandoned and workers would be offered contracts as independent contractors. Fred did not go to personnel to determine the plans, nor did he ask his boss. He heard the rumors and passed them on to his coworkers who panicked along with him. He accepted a job he was not enthusiastic about. After he was gone he learned the change in the company's provision of employee health insurance was minimal. They changed providers, not coverage.

When it was announced the company was being taken over by a conglomerate, Iris was beset with rumors. The word was that the multi-company group was cold, calculating, and inconsiderate of the human factor, that the employees were overwhelmed with paper work, and individual initiative was squelched. Iris could not stand not knowing. She had to get solid information to relieve her anguish and the turmoil surrounding her coworkers. When she saw the company's transition representatives she asked them what was going on and what the employees could expect in the way of changes. They told her what they knew and directed her to the head of the takeover team. She made an appointment and came back with the facts. The team leader was impressed with Iris's frank concern and briefed the team on how to be helpful to the employees. She also wrote a memo to the employees outlining the facts of the change. She honestly listed the areas that would feel the impact of change and let them know in which areas no decisions had been made. She set up a method for keeping the workers informed and told them where to go to get the information they needed to calm their concerns. Iris was comforted, as were her coworkers.

Ways to forestall rumors include the following:
1. Seek facts.
2. Debunk outlandish rumors.
3. Check out rumors with someone who knows the facts.

TACTIC # 18: KNOW RIGHT FROM WRONG

Seth felt so crummy about himself he lost his confidence in his ability and judgment. He did not know what to say to others and was convinced he could not get another job. He was not even sure he knew what was right and what was wrong. But he did know there were certain things he would not do, no matter how much he wanted to keep his job.

It would be easier if there were guidelines any employee could follow to stay out of trouble and on the side of the company and law and order. Unfortunately, there are so many shades between black and white that what is right and what is wrong is not always clear-cut. The newspapers are full of stories about employees and managers who are charged with white collar crimes, many protesting they did not know they were doing anything wrong or describing an escalation of action that started innocently and led to complications as they got in deeper than they thought they would with no clear way out of it. In the end their conduct appears calculated and their protests facile. Any employee, manager, or staff member can get involved in questionable, if not illegal activities, through faulty judgment, the desire to please, and the siren song of promotions and riches. Sometimes it is as simple as trying to cover up a mistake or as innocent as being in the wrong place at the wrong time and not having the strength or character to face the problem and make the appropriate corrections. The employees who bear up best in suspect circumstances are those who have a strong set of good values and a conviction about what they will and will not do to get along and get ahead. It also helps to have support from people who share those values and back the employee's decisions in controversial matters. These gurus can be relatives, mentors, friends, clerics, coworkers, former teachers, or some consortium of all of them.

Employees' abilities to make judgments wear down when they are constantly bombarded with ethical and legal dilemmas and the company policy is to live on the edge, never doing anything illegal, but stretching legality as far as it can possibly go. When everyone seems to accept a practice as right, it is difficult to take a stand that goes against the company. Sometimes it is necessary to consult someone objective who knows the law. Sometimes it is risky to do that as the employees have to implicate themselves if they are to tell the whole story. In far too many instances, employees have to rely on their own convictions to know where to draw the line.

Employees can disapprove of management's decisions and actions, have a different philosophy on how the business should be run, and disagree on priorities. This is not a question of right and wrong but an issue on how the job should be done. Employees may consider management foolish, ill-advised, stupid, and unthinking. That does not make what management is doing illegal or unethical. Employees can label management's approach "wrong," but that does not make it criminal or even harmful.

When employees' ethical standards clash with management's they are faced with a decision. Should they stand up for their beliefs, decide it is management's problem and not theirs, or look elsewhere for work? Again, this is the employee's personal and professional dilemma. The company policy can be right and still be ethically wrong in the opinion of the employee. But it is not necessarily illegal. One employee with a mission to hold a company to a moral standard may make a difference, but more likely will soon reach the limit of influence and find the position hopeless.

If management's actions are unfair or are contrary to written policies and procedures, the company's internal grievance policy is available. This does not promote popularity with the new administration, but, if circumstances leave employees feeling this is the only recourse, it is necessary.

If employees find new management's actions not only unacceptable, but illegal, other options are available. Employees can defend their rights through the Equal Employment Opportunity Commission (EEOC) or the National Labor Relations Board (NLRB). The EEOC is commissioned to investigate complaints related to age, sex, or race discrimination, file charges if the complaint is verified, and fight on behalf of the person bringing the discrimination complaint. The NLRB investigates accusations of unfair labor practices, which include unsafe working conditions, working too many hours without breaks, or compensation that does not meet minimum wage requirements. In each instance the employer is not allowed to dismiss the employee while the investigation is in progress. The Americans with Disabilities and Sexual Harassment acts provide further governmental and legal protection to employees.

Another legal, but risky, avenue is blowing the whistle on the operation. Whistle-blowers are protected by law. They cannot be fired or harassed while charges are under investigation. Theoretically, employees can safely make accusations and keep their jobs. The law, however, does not reflect what may actually happen. Whistle-blowers are not awarded promotions and are frequently fired for any reason an administrator can find. If there is no way to get rid of them they are ignored or branded as liars, crackpots, and trouble makers. They are accused of being resistant to change, trying to get even for imagined slights, or covering up their own guilt by maligning their employers.

If employees feel compelled to become whistle-blowers they are urged to take very good physical and emotional care of themselves because they need good health to sustain themselves. Whistle-blowing is difficult and takes a tremendous toll. No one but those who have gone through the process can really understand the anguish whistle-blowers feel when they are doing the right thing and their company tries to make them look as though they are in the wrong. Only employees who put themselves on the firing line can decide their limits and conclude whether or not the results are worth it.

Collin was glad he kept his job. His work went on as before and he had no problems with the new administration until he became aware that employees nearing retirement age were being laid off or let go in increasing numbers. Since he was approaching retirement himself, he started paying attention. The boss denied any systematic plan to unload long-time employees, citing cutbacks in some operations and the elimination of jobs. Collin did not challenge this but continued to study the problem and saw a pattern. He discussed this with long-time coworkers and former employees. They met to plan a strategy and decided they did not want to wait for a governmental agency investigation. They hired a labor lawyer and filed suit against the company. It was a long, hard, stressful, and time-consuming fight. It was also exciting and gave Collin and his group a sense of effectiveness and power. They were glad they did it even though there were many bad moments. Collin was fired while the action was in progress. Management watched him carefully and compiled a list of mistakes and other actions they labeled insubordinate. Reinstatement was ordered and Collin was offered early retirement. He gladly took it. Collin and his fellow workers felt their court case was worth the effort and aggravation, but they would never want to go through it again.

Josephine did not approve of the way new management was handling the company's money. Since this was a consumer based agency she thought the money should be put into services for the clients. The new administrator put money into remodeling, furniture, computers, and an upgrade of the facilities. Josephine stewed and complained. She succeeded in upsetting herself and her employer. In the end nothing changed and Josephine and her new boss keep their distance and continued their mutual disapproval. The money was not earmarked for clients, so the boss was not legally obligated to spend the money in any particular way. What the boss did went against what Josephine thought he should do, but it was within the law.

Bruce became aware that new management in his company was so concerned about cutting costs that they did not follow specifications in the products they manufactured. They advertised that certain elements were included in their goods, but they were not. Contracts calling for precise manufacturing methods and amounts were not followed. Customers were short-changed on the number and quality of items shipped to them. Bruce pointed this out to his new supervisor who listened with interest and said he would take care of it. When nothing was done, Bruce complained again. The supervisor suggested it was not Bruce's problem. When Bruce did not accept that, the supervisor told him to look the other way and do his job. Bruce would not do this. He took his concerns up through the hierarchy where he was offered explanations and excuses. He got nowhere except in trouble. His work evaluations started including charges of inefficiency, inability to work well with others, and difficulty in understanding and following instructions. He was put on probation. Bruce was hurt and demoralized, but not defeated. He reported his concerns to the organizations that received the inferior materials. To his amazement, this information was not universally welcomed and was not considered shocking (Bock, Clark & Cornett, 1973). Bruce got fired but his expose made the news. Others involved themselves in investigating the company's practices and management was indicted. Bruce was happy; right triumphed over wrong. He was awarded back pay and was exonerated, but remained jobless—unless one considers the talk show circuit gainful employment. But Bruce had weighed the potential consequences of action versus inaction prior to becoming so deeply involved and he knew the repercussions of passivity would have been worse for him personally than those of action.

Know what is right and what is wrong:

1. Tune into personal values and feelings of what is right and what is wrong.

2. Determine if the action is ill-advised or, in fact, illegal.
3. Talk to others who are bothered by the same problem.
4. Decide on a course of action.
5. Be prepared for recrimination and long-term stress.

CHAPTER FIVE REVIEW

1. Have conspiracies designed to get rid of the new manager been avoided?
2. Has energy been directed toward job goals?
3. Has the boss been briefed on what the employee does?
4. Are skills used to help the company succeed?
5. Is friendship spread among many coworkers rather than confined to one cliquish group?
6. Have personal and professional values been defined?

CHAPTER 6

CONTRIBUTE TO THE COMPANY'S SUCCESS

Lyle figured the boss got paid to be the boss and that he would not help her because then she would get ahead at his expense. He did not understand that he would also be making himself look good. Helping the boss does not mean employees are pandering (Eigen, 1990). It means they are contributing to the company's success.

TACTIC # 19: ADMIT MISTAKES, BUT FOLLOW UP BY DOING SOMETHING RIGHT

Kristen worked hard to avoid making mistakes. When she erred she tried to cover up by fixing it before it was discovered. Failing that, she would make excuses, blame others, or lie, saying she did not do it. She could not accept the fact her work was not perfect.

But all human beings make mistakes. That does not mean they have to advertise them. Some mistakes are inconsequential, some can be easily fixed, and some mistakes must be reported (Carnegie, 1936). Confession does not need to be accompanied by excuses and rationalizations. Such a reaction is defensive and sounds like an attempt to squirm out from under responsibility. However, if there is a reason for the mistake and it exonerates the employee, or the mistake was caused by a flawed procedure or machine, the experience becomes an opportunity to suggest measures to prevent future mistakes. If the boss suggests a plan for fixing the problem, employees proceed by expressing gratitude, following instructions, and reporting results.

Employees who fail to report their mistakes cause damage to themselves and to the company. A blunder that is not rectified compounds the problem by increasing harm to the company and making the employees more culpable. In the meantime, employees who know they are guilty spend distressful days fearing they will be found out, all the while imagining dire consequences. It is far better to inform the boss and take responsibility for an error than to live with the uncertainty of whether one will face repercussions if or when the mistake is discovered.

There are good and bad techniques for reporting mistakes. Mistakes are never funny when first presented. Employees want to appear serious and concerned and suggest a plan for fixing the problem that precludes it from happening again. As important as it is to confess the mistake, it is just as important for employees to not sell themselves out by presenting themselves as mistake-prone personalities or natural-born klutzes. Since the new boss does not know the employees, they will be taken at their word. Bad enough the new boss is meeting the employees in tense, negative circumstances; they do not need to make the situation worse by identifying themselves as "problem employees."

After admitting a mistake, the employee's next priority is to change his or her image. The best way to alter negative memories is to follow up with positive actions. Employees generate good impressions by doing something well, making contributions, solving problems, fixing mistakes, and letting the new boss know about it via memo, verbal report, or demonstration.

Irene thought if she presented herself as someone who was not a terrific worker her employers would not expect too much of her and they would be pleased when they discovered she could do the job. She was more than modest and tended to put herself down. When she made mistakes she acted as though this was typical. It was not that Irene made a lot of mistakes, it was just that she accepted them as the way she operated. She emphasized what she did wrong, rather than what she did right. The new boss accepted her self-evaluation, grew increasingly uneasy about Irene's work, and stopped assigning her responsibilities that required accuracy. Irene felt left out and quit her job because her situation depressed her.

Owen knew he goofed when he sent out a letter quoting the wrong price to a potential customer. The price was lower than the cost of manufacturing the product. When he explained it was his mistake and let the customer know the actual price, the customer became enraged and complained to Owen's new boss. Owen suggested that the company hold to the regular price, but offer the customer something extra to pacify him. He thought preferential service, a bonus for quantity buying, and discounts on subsequent orders should be suggested. The boss was not enamored with Owen's mistake, but did admire his creativity for getting the company out of it, and pleasing the customer at the same time. Owen made sure the boss knew of the customer's positive reaction to the proposal. He never made that mistake again.

To recap damage control on mistakes:
1. Take mistakes seriously.
2. Take responsibility. Do not make excuses or blame others.

3. Admit mistakes and have solutions ready.
4. Accept help and follow instructions for remedying mistakes.
5. Follow each mistake with actions that demonstrate ability.

TACTIC # 20: BE HELPFUL

Alicia was overtly helpful, eager to do what she could. She offered to run errands, bring coffee, supply aspirins. But she would not share credit. When she did something she wanted it known it was her accomplishment or idea. Once her boss proposed a plan that came from her. No one heard the end of it. Her fear that someone, especially her boss, would steal her ideas and take credit stymied her ability to work effectively. Because of her fear of being plagiarized, she was unwilling to put forth her thoughts. In her position she had to get her projects approved by her supervisor. But she would not tell her supervisor about her projects. Alicia was a great help as a person, but a failure as a helpful employee.

Employees and bosses are hired and kept because of what they can do. Employees who help their bosses look good are appreciated, but not always recognized for their contributions because some bosses take more than their share of credit for themselves. How bosses handle workers' contributions depends on their style. Some give employees thanks, recognition for their contributions, or mention them as contributors to the project. Employees do not know how the new bosses handle help until after the help is given. Even if the bosses are self-serving and take credit for their work, the employees are, nevertheless, making themselves useful and insuring job survival. If the bosses depend on the employees, the employees are achieving status for their abilities. Employees are, after all, hired to be active participants in the work effort.

The people who work for the company are expected to have goals consistent with the company's plans. Bosses and employees are more likely to accomplish their goals by working together than by working separately or at cross purposes. Employees want to attain recognition and reward, but need their bosses acclaim to accomplish this, so helping the boss and the company is part of what employees do to help themselves.

Bosses working with employees who are new to them want to know what the employees can do and how they can help them in their objectives. Bosses and employees want acceptance and appreciation, but since they do not know each other neither can rest on their reputations. Both need to prove themselves to each other. How well they work together in common endeavors is what counts.

Employees are not helpful to their bosses when they take ideas to higher authority or proceed with the development and implementation of their ideas without the bosses' knowledge. This is considered insubordination, not initiative.

New bosses appreciate help with the work and help with finding their way around. Employees who provide accurate and factual information on work in progress, community resources, political priorities, and troubleshooting techniques are seen as helpful.

It does not help anyone, especially the employees, to withhold information and create bottlenecks by refusing to participate in cooperative efforts. Such actions slow down production and interfere with efficiency. Recalcitrant employees cause redundancy since no one ever knows what they are doing. Contributing to team efforts, on the other hand, reaps respect and praise from coworkers and bosses.

James was upset with the way the new boss parceled out the work, so he decided he would do his job and keep to himself. He handled his own customers from beginning to end. He insisted they deal directly with him, not talking with the receptionist, not placing orders with clerks, and not working with the accounting department. He had his own telephone line, took all messages, prepared all orders, and collected the money. He did not trust the new boss or new employees to do anything right for his customers. He thought he was protecting them and himself. However, the employees who usually did the work he confiscated were angered because they knew he thought he could do it better. They complained. His customers liked the idea of only having to deal with one person at first but soon found James was hard to contact and no one else was available to help them. They complained. James was determined to protect his job and his consumers. Instead, he was viewed as odd. The boss could not keep James employed.

Martha was a friendly person so it was no effort for her to welcome the new boss, explain the office traditions, point out good places for lunch, and ask if she would like to accompany the group when they went out to eat. Martha was helpful and her helpfulness was expressed in a sincere and up-front way. The boss felt comfortable with her and soon was confiding in her.

In summary, to be helpful:

1. Give the boss the benefit of the doubt and present ideas and suggestions to see what he or she does with them.
2. Help the boss find his or her way around the new surroundings.
3. Help the boss look good.
4. Be a team player and help the boss and coworkers.

TACTIC # 21: LISTEN

Irving heard the same announcements regarding personnel reassignments and changed workday schedules that every other worker in the organization heard. Irving, however, insisted the company would never change. He decided to proceed as usual. Irving was not listening.

New bosses are hired to cut back on operations, strive for more efficiency, increase profit margins, get rid of deadwood, forge better community relations, increase product visibility, improve product quality, provide better services, change company direction, prevent bankruptcy, bring in new ideas, inspire creativity, boost productivity, or make sure the company complies with regulations. If employees listen, they quickly learn what they can do to fit in with and contribute to the success of the boss's mission (Wilder, 1994).

Employees learn the boss's intent by listening to what he or she says, noting what he or she asks about, and tuning in to his or her priorities. Employees are happiest and can be most productive when their goals coincide with those of the boss. If their ideas of what is right for the company are in sharp contrast to the boss's ideas they are in for a hard time. If they cannot bring themselves to help the boss achieve what he or she was hired to do, the employees are in a losing position because they will be unhappy at work or be unable to continue in their work. The sooner the employees understand the new boss's direction, the sooner they can stop speculating and get down to work. The more they know, the more effective they will be. Listening never stops because there is always more to know.

For example, listen in staff meetings. What can be learned from coworkers? What does the boss emphasize?

Listen to instructions. Instructions are given to make sure the job is done correctly, the employees understand the procedure, and the customers get the advertised projects. Instructions are not introduced to be ignored or used selectively. The boss uses instructions as a tool to unify and simplify an efficient effort.

Listen to coworkers. What have they learned about working effectively with the boss? Everyone does not need to learn everything firsthand. Employees can learn from the experiences of others. Information gives power (Simon, 1976).

Thelma wanted the new boss to understand how she did her job. Her good work was proven by the gratitude of her customers, her superior performance evaluations, and her promotions. She thought she had a lot she could teach the boss. The boss, however, was not interested in hearing what Thelma knew about providing service. She wanted to know what the employees did that brought in financial returns. The boss thought she had made her instructions very clear and could not understand why Thelma did not understand she was to help the company make a profit. Thelma did not listen because she could not believe the boss knew what she was talking about. If Thelma did not start listening, she and the boss could not continue working together.

Leon had a pet project. He wanted to pursue an area of research that past administrators thought unproductive. His repeated requests for research time and money brought repeated refusals. The new boss's message gladdened Leon's heart. The incoming manager made a stirring speech calling for creativity, new ideas, better ways to do routine things, and efforts that would achieve results in the long run. He asked the employees to bring him their suggestions no matter how far out they seemed. Here was a man Leon could work with! He could not wait to tell him about his long-delayed project. The new boss had the same reaction as the last several administrators. Leon was disappointed, especially after he had his hopes rekindled. But he listened and heard. He recognized the boss's address was meant to inspire the employees to be inventive, but not to stimulate them to go out on a limb. The boss wanted new ideas, but he wanted ideas he could cash in on in a hurry. Leon wanted to stay, so he tabled his favored project.

Joe's new boss told him he had better find something else he could do because she saw no reason to maintain his position. She thought his work redundant and the parts that were not could be done by a lower paid employee. Joe did not waste his time trying to get his boss to reconsider, but set out to find where in the company he might fit in. He located a department that needed help and asked for a transfer. He listened, followed instructions, and kept a job.

Listen and learn; to recap:

1. Listen to learn the boss's mission.
2. Listen for the boss's priorities.
3. Listen to the boss's plans for the company.
4. Listen to instructions.
5. Listen to coworkers' experiences with the new boss.

TACTIC # 22: CONTRIBUTE

Faith said they did not pay her to get along with people. She saved her social graces for her social life. She did her job. She did not make friends in the workplace. No one looked forward to seeing her. Other employees did not chat with her or share information.

An employee's major contributions are work-related. Workplace politics have nothing to do with the reason everybody is gathered together in one place. The political climate does not have much to do with whether or not the employees are contributing to the work effort, but it does have much to do with whether or not employees keep their jobs. Office politics focus on personality, being in the right place at the right time (Getting to the top, 1994), knowing the right people, and doing the right things. The major reason people lose their jobs is because of personality problems. Employees who contribute to the work environment through use of their positive personalities are seen in a more favorable light than those who have disagreeable personalities.

Although good work takes precedence, it is also taken for granted. Personality and politics are the extras that lead to high profile, influential contacts, and promotions.

Employees and bosses do better when they are comfortable with each other. Comfort is more readily attained when there is common ground. The same sex, age, and preferences go a long way toward establishing a feeling of commonality. Comfort is what contributes to bosses hiring people from the schools they attended, the part of the country they are from, their educational and work background, not to mention their religion, clubs, and interests. This is discrimination and it is illegal, but bosses are drawn to people who are a known factor. This factor is the familiar aspects of the employees and job applicants that give bosses the feeling that they know and understand these people because they know and understand their experiences. They sense that they can predict how they will do on the job because they can identify with the employee's background since it is similar to their experiences. This is why people get involved in specific organizations and charities, want to belong to certain clubs, and pride themselves in getting an education from selected schools. Recognition for contributions comes more easily when the employees fit in (Bowes, 1987).

Contributing to the community as a company representative is a major political plus in some companies. Public relations and marketing people are paid to capitalize on community need and match it to business contributions. Company employees who are volunteers at local organizations that serve to better the community are recognized for their contributions to the company and the community. If the employee's enthusiasm for a volunteer effort coincides with the boss's, so much the better. If the company wants to capitalize on the worker's extracurricular activities and contributions in the community, so be it. The employees get the satisfaction of helping out in an important volunteer undertaking and get recognition at work as well.

Work is only part of what goes on in the workplace and it is not the only thing that makes a difference. Contributions are also made by being part of the social activities. Somebody has to arrange parties, take collections, plan holiday observances, boost morale, and think of the employees who are in the hospital or are suffering personal tragedies. The company invests money and time into parties, banquets, ceremonies, and gifts because they want happy workers with good morale. They like to know that employees appreciate this and are willing to do their part to promote the activities that are planned to advance cohesiveness and good will.

Contributions in the workplace are made daily by employees who are cheerful, friendly, and thoughtful. Not only is this a meaningful contribution to the workers and the workplace, it enhances the stature of the employees in the eyes of those who appreciate their considerate attentions.

Amber was very active in the community. She was married to the president of the chamber of commerce, belonged to two community service organizations, and knew many of the area leaders. She worked hard as a volunteer in these associations and did so with her boss's blessing. Since her efforts entailed luncheon meetings, many telephone calls during work time, and the use of the computer and copier, her community liaisons were part of her work routine. The president of the bank where she worked saw her efforts as good for business. He encouraged other employees to participate in like manner.

Larry, who worked for the same bank, believed in preserving the environment. His community effort took time from his work and entailed use of the computer and the copying machine and put him in touch with highly placed people in the city. His efforts were not appreciated because he lobbied against developers and manufacturers he thought were ruining the environment. Since these people were significant bank customers, Larry was forbidden to work against the interests of the bank's depositors. He was told to pay attention to the job he was hired to do. He persisted, so the boss had his work monitored, documented how much time he put into his avocational interests, and gathered enough evidence to warn him that if his work time continued to be focused on his personal pursuits he would be fired.

Wendy did not have good luck with the new politics. Her boss expected the supervisors to stick around after work and talk about their day. Then they went out for drinks and dinner. Her boss wanted her top employees to be her social life. Wendy found this enjoyable at first. It was fun having the boss as a friend. But it got old when it cut into her needs to keep up with her other friends, her family, and her interests. She dropped out of the gathering and was cut off from the intimacy she had with her boss. She managed to keep her job, but always felt the boss resented her. When another opportunity in another company presented itself she grabbed it. Wendy did not like the political games that were apparently required by her new boss, so she did not continue those activities. But, she continued to do a good job and maintained her employment until she could find an agreeable alternative elsewhere.

Keep up the contributions:
1. Get along with others.
2. Make contacts at work and in the community.
3. Be part of the social aspects of the workplace.
4. Find a common ground with the new boss.
5. Look for clues to the boss's values.
6. Do not shirk work.

TACTIC # 23: GIVE FEEDBACK

Albert was in the dark and tired of it. He went to see his boss. In the course of getting more information Albert gave his boss the same kind of feedback he was looking for. They mutually caught up with what was going on.

The success of the employees, the bosses and the company is enhanced by teamwork and feedback. In other words, when people know what is going on—what is going well and what is not working—they have direction, reinforcement, and feel included. New bosses have lonely jobs and want feedback as badly as do the people they supervise. They get feedback from their supervisors, but that does not tell them how well they are doing in the most crucial part of their job. They want to know if they are succeeding with the employees, just as the employees want to know if they are succeeding with their bosses.

In fact, everybody wants feedback. Employees complain that the only time they receive feedback is when somebody has a complaint. That, of course, is significant input, but is only part of what is needed. Feedback includes the positive as well as the negative.

People love to get good feedback. Bosses are likely to continue to do what they get praise for doing, as are the workers. A "Well done!" "I enjoyed the presentation!" or "Great idea!" are terrific to hear, but not enough. If the new bosses make a popular contribution, do something specific that is appreciated by the workers, or achieve acceptance, they want to know. Some bosses ask for, but do not always get, the feedback they need. They are more likely to hear in general terms. The employees miss an opportunity when they are not specific because, if they are not told, bosses are unable to pick out what they did that pleased the staff and what displeased them. They are unwilling to ask in detail and employees are unsure whether they should critique the bosses' actions in detail. But bosses need to hear good and bad. Since the bad can be discouraging, it should be coupled with the good news. That gives a complete picture. Feedback is appropriate when the following occurs:

1. *The new procedure works well.* Once employees are accustomed to a new way to do an old thing and it is going well, the boss wants to know. There may be glitches and the boss needs to know that too.

2. *The employees respond positively to the new administration.* The response may be good overall, but if some specific problems persist the boss needs to be told so those problems can be addressed through further explanation or

change or the workers can be helped to understand that this is the way it is at this time.

3. *The employees accept the new directions.* It is good news when the employees have success with a new system. If the workers have suggestions for making the new directions work better, the boss needs to be given the proposals in hopes that he or she will consider trying them or explain why it is not feasible.

4. *Morale is good.* The boss is thrilled to know that he or she did something that increased or maintained morale. Not as thrilling, but equally consequential, is providing information on what is damaging morale.

5. *Production is good.* When the boss experiences success in production he or she feels more confident that he or she can correct hold-ups in production after being informed about them.

6. *Quick action is needed.* When the boss does not understand that an emerging problem requires immediate attention, it is positive feedback to report the urgency of the situation. Letting the boss make critical mistakes is not good feedback.

7. *The boss does something right.* Employees do not want to pass up a chance to let the boss know he or she did something impressive.

8. *Personnel changes went well.* Personnel changes are touchy, so if the changes make most of the employees happy, the boss deserves the good news. Unhappiness also needs to be reported, even when everybody knows there is nothing that can be done about it.

9. *The boss makes a presentation.* All of the employees are not going to like all of any given presentation. The boss wants to know what was well received and what was not.

10. *There is a recurring problem.* In established companies there is a standard way to manage problems that recur. The

question to ask is, was the problem handled effectively and efficiently in the past or is this the boss's opportunity to come up with a new way?

11. *Employees have a hard time with a particular change.* Employees embrace change when they see immediate benefits. If there is nothing in it for them, it is just more unwanted change. The new boss may be able to make the change more palatable through clear explanation, offering rewards for extra work, or giving leeway somewhere else. But the boss cannot make any accommodations if he or she does not know what is going on (Latting, 1992).

12. *The boss asks about a procedure.* The thing to ascertain is this: Is the question a directive or a comment? Employees do not have to figure that out all by themselves. Asking is giving feedback on whether or not the boss wants something researched, changed, or left alone.

Feedback is one part of good communication. There is the story of the 34th president of the United States, Dwight David Eisenhower (1890-1969), and the White House squirrels. He played a lot of golf on the White House lawn and commented on the squirrels getting in his way. The Secret Service employees did not give him feedback. They took what he said as an order and did away with the squirrels. President Eisenhower was surprised at the sudden disappearance of all the squirrels and amazed at the Secret Service employees' reaction. The story made the newspapers. Squirrel-lovers were incensed.

Without feedback, employees can get into this same kind of trouble. A boss who complained about being bothered by a certain supplier was chagrined to learn all business ties were cut with that company. The boss's irritation with the supplier meant only that the supplier was difficult, not that the relationship should be terminated.

A boss who thought she was doing everybody a favor shortened the lunch break so employees could leave work a half hour early. She was pleased to know that she made the employees happy, but she also needed to know that many employees found a longer lunch break more important than leaving work early.

Daniel listened to his boss, decided he was to discontinue services to one area of the community, and proceeded to inform the rest of the employees. They were dumbfounded and could not believe the directive could be true. They refused to act on it. Daniel was forced to return to the boss and restate what he heard. The boss clarified and told him he had it wrong. He had been musing out loud that he wished he could, but he knew he couldn't as it probably flew in the face of some regulation. Daniel had to retract what he told the employees.

The new boss hired another person to help with the workload. Everybody was glad to share their work with him. That was not a problem. The problem arose because there was a shortage of available office space. The new employee was arbitrarily assigned an office with one of the senior staff members. The boss made the decision based on his observation of whose customers came to the office. It seemed to him that this particular employee had less need for a private office. His decision satisfied him, but he did not explain the basis for it to anyone. He thought it was going well because he overheard the twosome working out arrangements for who would put what where, and what each could offer in the way of decorative items. To him it was no big deal, so he was surprised when a member of his staff told him the worker was unhappy, felt there was discrimination in the decision, and did not understand why she was picked to share an office. His explanation of his perception of office use based on direct customer contact was discounted. He had not made a study to see if his impression was factual. The staff member who gave him feedback suggested he rethink his decision and base office sharing on seniority. He did, apologized, and kept a valuable employee from active discontent.

It is good to give feedback under these circumstances:
1. On employees' reactions and how the reactions are affecting their job performance.
2. On the good and the bad. But try to couple bad with good.
3. When the boss doesn't recognize there is a problem.
4. When employees are pleased with the boss's actions and decisions.
5. When exceptions need clarification.

CHAPTER SIX REVIEW

1. Are employees helping the boss get acquainted in the workplace and the community?
2. Are ideas and suggestions shared with the boss?
3. Is the boss being heard when he or she explains what he or she wants the employees to do?
4. Are contributions to the community and the social aspects of the job used to enhance the company's standing in the area?
5. Does the boss know the extent of the employees' work responsibilities?
6. Are workers adapting to the new boss's priorities?
7. Does the boss get feedback so the boss knows what is going on and the employees are sure they understand what is said?

DEMONSTRATE PROFICIENCY

Belle was caught in an "invisible entrapment" (Waitley, 1980: 47). She was worried, anxious, and knew she could not cope with all the changes in the chain of command. She did not recognize the positive actions she could take to show her favorable contributions and characteristics to the new or reassigned supervisors and employees.

There is hope and hopelessness, positive and negative, good and bad, happiness and despair, contentment and discontent. Every horrible situation has something good somewhere. It is a matter of choice. Focus can be on the awful or the good. Realistically, new management is not 100 percent terrific, but it is not 100 percent catastrophic either. It is possible for employees to build on what is satisfactory. Those who say, "I can't," engineer their own failure. "I can," augurs success.

TACTIC # 24: COMMUNICATE WITH COWORKERS

Genese knew her job, but she also knew and enjoyed people. She was tuned in to their moods and never hesitated to talk to people. She was communicative without being garrulous. She knew how to say the right thing at the right time. She was a positive person and elicited positive responses from others. This special skill stood her in good stead with the new workers and new management.

Some people's best friends are their coworkers. Since they socialize as well as work with their buddies they have a lot of communication, to the chagrin of their spouses, who complain of constant shop-talk. When husbands and wives feel left out and when the talk is made up of slanderous gossip or anxiety-producing predictions, the talk is hurtful instead of helpful.

Communication with coworkers that provides necessary information, such as reports on what one worker is doing that affects other workers, is productive. Conversations directed toward helping each other and working together are positive exchanges. Supportive statements, individual concerns, and shared work knowledge and expertise are helpful. Memos and observations are good ways to keep up, but talking with other people in the workplace gives the big picture.

People who listen and share information are better liked than those who shun company and are uncommunicative. Being liked is an advantage in all work situations, particularly during times of new management. New managers look favorably upon people who know how to get along with others. They are impressed with old employees who get acquainted with new employees and share knowledge, abilities, routines, and information. Old employees who do this are seen as good facilitators who should be kept on the job. People who are approachable, have something to offer, and are willing to talk are perceived as friendly, helpful, open, and caring (McQuaig, McQuaig & McQuaig, 1981). Workers who do not reach out are labeled standoffish, snobbish, or uncaring.

When there is nothing to communicate, employees can fall back on small talk and continue good communication. Talking even when there is nothing to say keeps the communication lines open and makes it easier to talk about work related problems at another time. Small talk fills time during hellos and good-byes, breaks, and when waiting for a meeting to begin, and is composed of friendly inquiries about the employee, activities, weather, current events, and work in progress.

Arlene was everybody's secretary and had to communicate with all the employees. She helped the new employees feel comfortable by explaining what she did and how quickly they could expect their work returned to them. She accommodated herself to them by asking their preferences in form and style. She helped them compose their letters to meet the professional standards of the company. She managed to become a favorite of the new administration.

Keith, the curmudgeon (as he was known to old and new employees alike) was not a warm, friendly, or welcoming person. He did his job and did not want to be bothered. The old boss and employees were accustomed to him, knew he did his work well, and left him alone. The new boss and employees saw him as a difficult person. They tried to talk to him and felt rebuffed and their resentment grew. It was not only that he did not communicate, but that he sent a negative message that he was inaccessible. Nobody went out of their way to try to keep him on the job.

In communicating with coworkers remember the following:

Communicate with coworkers for:
- √ mutual support,
- √ sharing of knowledge and information,
- √ coordinating work,
- √ helping each other, and
- √ keeping up positive relationships.

Reach out to new employees to:
- √ demonstrate cooperation,
- √ coordinate activities, and
- √ develop routine verbal exchanges.

TACTIC # 25: TACKLE PROBLEMS

Edwin was timid about making suggestions. He was hindered by lack of self-confidence. When he saw a solution to something, he thought it was so obvious everyone else could see it too. He did not want to embarrass himself by presenting stupid ideas. Because he was reticent, his old boss never asked him to participate in problem solving. The new boss had no preconceived expectations about Edwin and engaged him directly in tackling problems. Edwin was fired up to find that his ideas were not only acceptable, but sought after. His expectations about himself changed (Chapman, 1982).

Work problems are part of the worker's responsibilities. When new management and the accompanying changes are resented it is easy to let that resentment get in the way of problem solving. There is often an attitude that goes something like this: New management caused the problems so they can live with them or fix them. This is not constructive because workers appear ineffective and incompetent if they act out that attitude. Any employee who elected to keep the job made the choice to take care of the job. Not addressing problems is not doing the job.

New management does the best it can do, but it cannot do all that has to be done. That is why there are employees. It is up to the employees to carry out the work and problem solve when defects occur.

When a changed system does not work out, particularly if the change did not seem necessary, gleeful reactions are experienced by many workers. The desire to say, "I told you so," is hard to dismiss. Nevertheless, tackling the problem with grace and an aura of helpfulness is to the worker's benefit. Workers who can solve problems and do so willingly and professionally make a good impression.

When workers go the extra mile to solve problems, such as by staying at work until a difficulty is remedied or working harder to meet a deadline, they develop a can-do reputation and become an important resource to the company.

Bosses are happy when they have employees who can fix things and keep the work flowing. Employees who go to the boss for advice on every single thing are a concern to the bosses because they worry what would happen if something had to be done and the boss was not available for consultation. Bosses feel secure when they are able to identify employees who are responsible and capable and can keep things running. Reports to the boss after the fact are successful when the results were successful.

Rose did not like the new administrator and saw him as ineffective and nonsupportive. She blamed him for anything that went awry and confronted him with everything that came up. When mail was returned to the office as undeliverable she never remedied the problem, but passed it on to the boss who politely told her to correct it and mail it out again. She did the same thing when there were complaints about the office temperature, forcing the boss to take care of the issue. Rose always asked the boss to handle any situation, no matter what petty matter came up. He was well aware she was pestering him with minor problems just to let him know the organization was not going well.

Marie saw a communication breakdown when the new manager arrived and several new department heads were hired. She had trouble doing her work as she was not notified of the opening and closing of the customer's files. New customers meant a bonus for the salesperson. Lapsed customers meant Marie was to contact them to determine if there was a problem. Without notification she could not do her job and the sales staff did not get their money. She knew the new employees did not know the system. She cleared up the issue by writing out a notification procedure and asking the boss if there was agreement. After the boss approved, the written procedure was sent throughout the system and an effective method was again in place.

Demonstrate problem solving skills by considering the following:

1. Address the problem, not who is to blame for the problem.
2. Demonstrate problem-solving ability.
3. Make the solution look easy.
4. Keep work current so rapidly occurring problems can be addressed.
5. If possible, solve problems without going to the boss.

TACTIC # 26: DEMONSTRATE FLEXIBILITY

Jeremy could not be faulted for his dedication to his work. He was efficient, accurate, and hard working. But his dedication was limited to his assigned jobs. He was impatient with work he considered to be unrelated to what he was doing, and he saw the customers as irritants. He was a model when it came to production, but impossible when flexibility was required.

Flexibility is key to any workers who want to remain employed in a company undergoing change. Although inertia fights change (Hampton, Summer & Webber, 1987), it can be overcome by looking forward to learning new habits, other ways of doing the same old thing, and exciting ventures into the unknown.

Overcoming inertia means adapting to the new manager's demands. Depending on the new boss's mandate and philosophy, changes can come immediately and rapidly or be delayed while the boss studies the operation. But there will be changes, probably in who reports to whom, the way paperwork is handled, where the office is located, how reporting is managed, when staff meetings are held, and anything else the boss deems appropriate. The new boss brings knowledge from past experiences and applies them to the present reality. The new boss's experiences are different from the employees'. There is a reason for that. Change is the mandate.

The new boss has to do many things early on. This person has to become personally acquainted with the work and the workers, answer to a new boss, and fulfill the commission for which he or she was hired. The new boss has to look like he or she knows what he or she is doing. This individual needs the employees' help.

Change is disruptive, but lack of change is boring. The arrival of new management provides a worker with a chance to get out of a rut, learn new skills, and find ways to improve the product. There is new excitement in the job. The boss enjoys seeing this spark. When employees feel good about their work, the boss feels good about them.

Flexibility means helping out until jobs get defined. There will be some work that has to be done and employees who willingly pick up the slack earn respect and recognition. In downsizing situations, chaos is the given. Employees are expected to be flexible and dig in to help out. It means coming in early, staying late, missing breaks, accommodating urgent projects, and responding to emergencies. Change and urgency come fast in today's market because bosses move around, new technology is endemic, and speed is the order of the day. Flexibility is not just nice, it is necessary. The ability to work with ambiguity and uncertainty—to improvise—is a key to success. Companies cannot wait for their employees to get caught up. Employees who learn to be flexible and deal with change are the employees who survive and do well.

Melinda was moved to an office with no windows. She saw it as a loss in stature. She learned later that her new boss planned to transfer her to a more responsible job in another department so her unsatisfactory office assignment was unimportant in lieu of her upcoming advancement.

Judith hated mornings. The new boss opened and closed the office a half hour earlier. Judith did not comply. She arrived late and, although she left late, the boss could not adjust to Judith's cavalier attitude about the starting time. She and her boss did not get synchronized. This seemingly minor rigidity on Judith's part was an irritation to her boss for as long as they worked together. And it was longer than the boss wanted it to be.

Flexibility is a job skill that may be enhanced by remembering the following:

1. The decision to stay on the job is a decision to adjust to change.
2. Minor procedural changes are easy to accommodate.
3. The boss has to produce to find favor with his or her boss.
4. Change needs a chance.
5. There are advantages in the changes.
6. Change is stimulating and an opportunity to learn.
7. Do what has to be done, step outside assigned duties, and help out in emergencies.
8. Flexibility should be recognized as a crucial job skill.

TACTIC # 27: FOREGO REQUESTS FOR SPECIAL FAVORS AND STAY ON THE JOB

Jana took care of her elderly mother. When her mother had to go to the doctor, Jana took time off during work hours. The company gave her the freedom to do this provided she paid back the time. She planned to continue the same arrangement with her new employers.

This type of special arrangement worked out amicably with the former boss, but may not set well with new management. The new bosses do not know the employees, do not want to make special exemptions, and do not want to be bothered with problems. Employees who have legitimate responsibilities outside of work and willingly work around them by putting in extra time, scheduling appointments late in the day, and using accrued sick or vacation leave, expect to make the same arrangements with new management as they made with the old. But it is not the same as before. Old employees with new managers do not want to call attention to themselves as people who need individual consideration. Even though the bosses are sympathetic, they are also there to run a business. If there are layoffs, among the first to go are people who present problems, no matter how justifiable the problems may be. Exceptions such as unusual events, emergencies, and person-specific work styles are suspect with new managers. They do not know the employees and feel they are being asked for something they would rather not consider until they know the staff better.

Eccentric work styles that embody starting the day from home, saving up expense sheets for six months prior to submitting them for payment, disappearing during the work day, not being where scheduled, and taking vacation time without planning ahead make new bosses nervous.

If personal emergencies interfere with the workday, employees are urged to consider all options before going to the boss. What can other family members with more time and established jobs do to help out? Can they take the child to the doctor, rush the pet to the vet, stand in line to pay the traffic ticket? Employees presented with no alternative but to take care of the problems themselves have no choice. They have to explain the situation to the boss, but can reassure the boss by adding how they plan to make up or cover their work in their absence, how they can be reached when not in the work place, and how long the special circumstance will continue. Then they keep to their side of the bargain, updating the boss at regular intervals, and expressing gratitude for the consideration.

New bosses do not want to be mean, but they want to be tough. They do not want their bosses to see them as pushovers or have other employees accuse them of favoritism. The old peeve that can be captioned by the phase, "If I do it for one I'll have to do it for everybody," is a constant concern of employers.

Vera wanted to put off her involvement in the change-over. Since she was not for it, she decided to avoid it. She scheduled her vacation to coincide with the new boss's arrival. She recognized her mistake when she returned and struggled to catch up.

When new bosses arrive at a new job, they are learning the ropes and making decisions about who does what and why. Any employee who is not present at that crucial interval does not participate in the start-up. They are not part of the boss's learning process. If work can go on without them the boss wonders why they are needed.

The boss develops new working habits, alliances, and communication systems in a new setting. Once established, it is not easy for latecomers to stake out their place in the loop. Patterns are set and absent employees' places in the organization get passed over.

If there is any choice, delay vacation plans and put off elective medical leave until work with the new boss has commenced and the boss and the employees know each other better. If there is no choice, employees can play catch-up by talking with fellow employees prior to returning to work and asking about work assignments and pressures. Prepared questions that follow up on work in progress and work changes help to sidetrack complaints about the changes. Employees prepare themselves for meeting the new boss by going in early their first day back, taking inventory of their work status, and getting organized. Then they are ready to present themselves to the boss, report on the condition of their work, and thank the boss for working around them. Telling the boss they are set for work as their vacation gave them renewed dedication, or their sick leave resulted in good health and stamina, is exactly what new managers want to hear.

Denise had trouble making ends meet. She determined she would do fine financially if she took a second job. She found a part-time position, but it required morning availability.

Denise saw no reason why she could not work her full-time job afternoons and evenings. She would stay later and work after everybody went home. The first time she met her new boss, she proposed flex-time for herself. She was refused because flexible working hours were not a policy with the company. Denise was furious. She knew she could do her job and do it better because there would be no interruptions during the evening hours. She argued, but the boss stood firm. She stomped off in bad humor. He saw her as petulant and a person who was only concerned about getting her own way. She did redeem herself by doing her job well, however, and when there were deadline crunches, Denise got to work the overtime and earn the extra money.

Jay saved for years for his trip to England. His ancestors were English and he wanted to study and record his family genealogy. Appointments were made and tickets paid for when word came there would be a new boss. Jay did not want to cancel his plans or lose his money. He was upset, but went anyway and worried most of the time. He was so distressed he called every coworker he could as soon as he returned to town. He wanted to know about the changes and the new boss's agenda. He went to his office over the weekend, got organized, read the memos, and reoriented himself. He was ready to dig in when he officially reported in. He made a point of meeting the new boss, relating the status of his work, emphasizing how eager he was to be productive, asking if there were instructions, and got down to business. He took longer to adjust to the changes than did his coworkers because he was not there in the beginning. But he applied himself and was soon working alongside the new boss as easily as were the other staff members.

It was not Rebecca's fault she was in a car accident and hospitalized. She was in intensive care, so her new boss could not consult with her about the state of her work. The boss relied on others to explain what Rebecca did. She needed their help to get Rebecca's work completed. Since Rebecca was away from work for an extended period of time, the boss stopped thinking of the work as Rebecca's work. When Rebecca returned part-time, there wasn't much for her to do. She had to be assertive to reclaim her job. The boss continued to talk to people who had taken over while she was out. Rebecca was hurt and angry, but persistently reclaimed her job. Only when she returned full-time did she reestablish herself as a contributing staff member. It took time for the boss to recognize Rebecca as the one who was responsible for the job. Rebecca was helped by her coworkers, who were pleased to get rid of the extra work.

If personal responsibilities and time off interfere with work, remember:

1. New management means not taking previous privileges for granted.
2. Good work habits should be established before asking for special allowances or taking vacations.
3. The boss wants to know how the job will be completed and how long an exception is needed.
4. Bosses like to be appreciated when they grant favors.
5. After being away, to play catch-up by calling coworkers and reporting early to get organized.
6. To check with the boss upon return and reassure him or her of a healthy mind and body that is ready to work.

TACTIC # 28: VOLUNTEER

Quincy wanted to do his work and be left alone. He allowed his "work to interfere with his job" (Donnelly, 1992: 91). In his isolation he did not learn, he did not get ahead, he did not volunteer.

Volunteering is not simply a nice thing to do. Employees volunteer to show off their abilities, to indicate their interests, to take charge of whatever work and particular assignments come their way, to appear useful and cooperative, to create a good impression, to look ambitious, to learn, to increase their value to the company, to augment their image, to meet people, and to gain a more prominent profile. By volunteering, they have more control over what they do. They do not have to wait for assignments, they select them, all the while defining their role in the company. They demonstrate that they can get along with different people and function well in a variety of circumstances.

Employers notice employees who volunteer when they demonstrate dimensions the bosses did not see previously. They note the volunteers can learn new skills and do not avoid work. Bosses are grateful to workers who volunteer for short-term projects, such as making a speech, devising a form, typing a grant, planning a party, orienting a new employee, writing a policy, working on a special assignment, assisting a move, trying out a new system, or devising a faster process. Short-term volunteering brings quick results and immediate appreciation. Volunteering for long-term projects takes more thought as the job soon becomes the employee's. Later efforts to get out of the job can erase all the good will created when the person took on the project.

There are some caveats. Employees who volunteer and then do not do the job are looked on with disfavor, as are employees who neglect their assigned work to concentrate on their volunteer duties.

Grace did not volunteer for anything. When she saw problems she complained about them, but made it clear it was not her job to fix them. She expected the new boss to take care of such failings and leave her out of it. Trouble-shooting was not in her job description. It was not part of her job. She had no experience with it and already had enough to do. All this was true. The new boss did not disagree with her position. But he hated to see her coming because she always described difficulties, never had suggestions for solutions, and never volunteered to help out.

Max volunteered frequently when he saw something that needed doing. He did not neglect his responsibilities while he worked on the special arrangements for the annual meeting and agreed to take his turn at clipping pertinent articles from the newspaper. Volunteering was a bonanza for him as he rubbed elbows with the officers of the company when he worked on the annual meeting, and he learned more about the company when he gave his attention to applicable news articles. He liked it so much, in fact, he volunteered for another year. The new boss liked Max's attitude. Max liked the benefits of volunteering. It enlarged his area of influence and made his job more interesting.

To summarize:
1. Get a wanted job by volunteering.
2. It looks good to volunteer.
3. Volunteer when a need is seen and before volunteers are requested.
4. Volunteer for short-term assignments.

TACTIC # 29: CONCENTRATE ON THE CUSTOMER

Preston did not believe in suffering alone. He told everybody, including the customers, about the incompetence of the bosses and the lack of fairness inherent in the new policies and procedures. He liked their support, but these people could not help him keep his job.

Change is hard on everybody, including a company's customers. They appreciate changes that bring faster service, lower prices, and better quality. They do not appreciate changes that connect them to employees who do not know what is going on, or do not care, or do not respond to their needs. Change is something for employees, not customers, to handle.

Employees who transfer their distress onto the customers are not doing a good job for the company or for themselves. It alarms the customers and does not help the employees. If good service stops, customers stop doing business with the company.

Customers do not care who is in charge, they want and deserve service.

Minor changes need not affect customers at all, however, changes that are minor to workers are frequently major changes to customers when the changes involve telephone numbers, locations, procedures, and people.

It takes customers longer to adjust to change because they are not exposed to the changes every day. The employee's responsibility is to have patience and guide the customers through the procedures and introduce them to the new people and the new policies. Employees who have heard the same complaints and questions again and again need to remind themselves that the complaints and questions are new for the customers. Rolling the eyes, sighing, and allowing an edge in the voice are not helpful mannerisms. Customers rightly expect to be accommodated, have their complaints heard, and promises of adjustments fulfilled. If they ask, they should be put through to supervisors or given names and addresses if they want to write their grievances.

If there are no customers, there is no job.

Olivia liked the excitement of change. Her positive attitude toward change and experience with change helped her help the customers. She saw change as a learning opportunity. Working for a large bureaucracy she had all the changes one would ever need to become expert in the process. She was exposed to continual changes as managers came and went and new solutions were tried on old problems. She was the perfect candidate for the opening in the customer service department because of her patience, enthusiasm, and sense of perspective about change. She liked the diversity in the job and found her niche in making customers happy (Suriano, 1994). She was an expert in understanding and explaining new protocols to confused and upset customers.

In contrast, Jeanette had a hard time with the change but recognized it was also hard for the customers. She did not follow the new procedure with ease. But she wanted to do it correctly and she wanted the customers treated right. Although it was awkward, and the customers complained, they understood from Jeanette that it was a permanent change to make the delivery of services more efficient. She was learning, just as she knew the customers were. She did not complain, but went out of her way to demonstrate they would be taken care of and well taken care of. She adjusted to the changes as did her customers. They all got through it with minimal distress.

Chris was miserable with the changes instigated by the new boss. He felt they interfered with the way he did his job. He was unhappy and made a point of explaining to everybody why nothing was working right. It was his job to answer the telephone. Since responsibilities were in the process of reassignment, he did not always know who did what. He made this clear to anyone who called the company and connected them with anybody rather than look up the new assignments. Customers were frustrated and took their business elsewhere. Chris saw this as confirmation of his belief that people did not like the changes. It was the new boss's fault. He hoped this would make it necessary for the company to return to the way things were done in the past. The new boss did not consider that option. Since business was slow he decided they did not need as many people to answer the telephone and instead needed more direct sales people. Chris got fired. A sales person got hired.

Give customers good service by noting the following:
1. Work problems are the employees' problems, not the customers' problems.
2. Letting the customers know about the employees' distress does not help the customers or the employees.
3. Good service is all that counts.
4. Employees who help customers help themselves.

5. Help customers through change by:

√ giving assistance as needed,

√ showing patience,

√ labeling the change an effort to give better service,

√ keeping personal discontent private,

√ accepting complaints without trying to capitalize on them,

√ being cheerful and upbeat about the changes.

√ listening,

√ not rushing the customer's adjustment,

√ helping the customers feel secure, and

√ being positive about the new people with whom the customers will be involved.

CHAPTER SEVEN REVIEW

1. Is positive communication maintained with coworkers?
2. Is there outreach to include new employees?
3. Are problems tackled promptly and eagerly?
4. Is change recognized as stimulating and an opportunity to learn?
5. Is asking for exceptions and favors approached cautiously?
6. Do employees volunteer so they can learn and get a chance to do more of what they enjoy?
7. Are times away from work delayed until the boss gets to know the employee?
8. Are the company's customers helped through the company's changes?

SUPPORT THE NEW MANAGER

Allison was satisfied with her first job. It was not a job she wanted to toil at forever, but she liked it and thought she did all right. When a change in management occurred, she made no effort to become acquainted with the new boss and the new procedures. She decided if the new situation did not appeal to her she would leave. Her manner made her position clear to her new boss who was ready to see her go so he could hire someone who wanted to belong to and participate in the newly reorganized company. The boss made her leave sooner than she had planned.

The boss is hired to produce and cannot do so without the help of the employees. As insecure as employees may be, so are the bosses, but they cannot show it because their job is to lead. They must demonstrate that they can get more out of the available resources than did the previous boss. Since employees are a company's most important resource, they are crucial to the accomplishment of management and company goals. The bosses want a satisfied and motivated group of employees (Lorsch, Baughman, Reece & Mintzberg, 1978). Their jobs depend on it.

The new boss may or may not be aware of what the employees underwent prior to the change in leadership. Whether or not the boss is aware, this person knows he or she did not cause whatever happened before he or she arrived. The new boss is not responsible for any hurt and discomfort the employees experienced. All the new boss wants to do is work to achieve the company's goals. He or she needs the employees' help and has much in common with them. Like the employees, the new boss wants to get along, be accepted, do good work, succeed, and keep his or her job.

TACTIC # 30: LET THE BOSSES KNOW THEIR JOBS ARE SAFE

Ed had an ego the size of Alaska. He was talented, knew it, and, furthermore, thought he could do anything. He was turned down for his new boss's job. The company opted to bring in someone from outside who had a record of success at that level of supervision. But the real reason Ed was not chosen was because he gloated. His favorite sport was rubbing it in when he was right, and he was right a lot of the time.

Secure and experienced bosses who know their businesses well are confident of their ability and possess good self-esteem. They do not worry that the people they work with are after their jobs. If they see ambitious workers, they encourage them. Bosses who marginally won their jobs over other contenders, who have not had much experience, and who feel unsure of themselves are uneasy around anyone they suspect wants their jobs, could do their jobs, expresses interest in their jobs, or does work of such good quality that others note the worker's exceptional ability.

The secure boss knows what to do; the insecure boss needs the employees' help; both want the employees' backing.

Employees are quick to notice when their bosses are threatened by them. There is some satisfaction in seeing discomfort in an unwanted boss, but in the end it does not pay off for the employees. Bosses who feel shaky try to make the employees uneasy through criticism, dismissal of accomplishments, emphasis of mistakes, taking credit for their work, avoiding them, questioning their work, and being disagreeable. This is unfair; nevertheless, it is a problem employees cannot ignore in the hope it will go away.

One thing employees can do is reassure their insecure bosses that they are not after their jobs. A forthright statement might work, but finding a way to fit it in without sounding threatening or out-of-line may be difficult. There are many ways to say the same thing. Employees can tell their bosses they are glad the bosses have the job as they would not want to have the bosses' responsibilities. Bosses are pleased to hear if the employees like their jobs. If a boss feels vulnerable, this news is very welcome. Bosses like to know that employees like having a boss who does his or her job so they can do the jobs they want to do.

Employees who are interested in advancement are safe in relating that information to their boss if it is in a different department or out of the company. The boss may be so relieved to hear such information he may help the employees get what they want. This is politics. The boss gets support from the employees and employees get help from the boss (Carr, 1989).

The new boss knew Diane, a long-time employee, had applied for his job prior to his being hired for the position. He was brought in from outside and needed her ability and help. She gave this to him, but at the same time one-upped him every chance she got. She was particularly competitive when others were around. It was apparent Diane thought she could do the job better than her boss. He put up with it as long as he needed Diane's knowledge. When he no longer was dependent on what she knew he eased himself away from her. It was evident one of them would have to leave. It was not the boss.

Rick was a competent worker. He did his job well, had a good education, handled himself well, and was respected by all who worked with him. The new boss thought he did too well, saw him as a threat, and as a consequence picked on him. She jumped on Rick's mistakes, criticized him when he used his own judgment, and worked at making him feel insecure. Rick was about ready to quit when the boss raged she knew he could never do her job. This gave Rick the information he needed. He said he also knew he could not, as he did not have the administrative skills. He did not want to deal with personnel problems and reports. But he did want to do a good job in his present position. He let his boss know he needed her help. The boss believed him. Her attitude toward Rick and her treatment of him changed perceptibly.

Let the boss know his or her job is safe because:

√ the employee has other goals,

√ the responsibility is not wanted,

√ the present job is satisfactory, and

√ administration is not the employee's forte.

Reassure the boss by:

√ not complaining about the job,

√ asking for help and advice,

√ explaining interest in other jobs,

√ giving support, and

√ telling the boss he or she is doing a great job.

There is evidence the boss is suspicious that the employee wants his or her job if:

√ the boss avoids the employee,

√ the boss questions the employee's work and ability,

√ the boss uses the employee's ideas as his or her own,

√ the boss criticizes the employee in an attempt to demoralize, and

√ the boss withholds information from the employee.

TACTIC # 31: CHECK WITH THE BOSS

To make a good impression on the new boss, Ellen decided to wow him by instigating and completing a project that would elevate her to star employee. This was not a good plan. The boss kept wondering what Ellen was up to. By the time she was ready to spring her surprise, he had such a mind-set against her work habits there was little she could have done to counteract his suspicions.

Bosses want to feel useful and important. They want to be the boss. But there is more. Two college professors reported in a 1993 study that ingratiating behavior gave employees a four-to-five percent advantage over the workers who relied solely on job performance for getting ahead (Odom, 1993). The "get along to get ahead" adage appears to be true.

Eric did not want to admit he needed help because he thought it a sign of weakness. Rather than ask his boss, he asked everybody else. When he was not sure about an assignment he gathered opinions and forged ahead the best he knew how. If it turned out wrong he blamed his sources of information. Repeatedly, the boss asked him if understood his assignment and urged him to ask if he needed help or was not clear about the task. Eric assured the boss he knew just what to do and he could handle it. Something was invariably neglected or some part of the job did not turn out right. After a few of these fiascoes the boss stopped asking Eric to do anything that mattered. He was relegated to routine work that did not require thought or judgment. Eric was happy he no longer got assignments that frustrated him. The boss was relieved he did not have to deal with Eric or worry about where he would goof up next.

Angie had more work than she could handle. She asked her boss to help her set priorities since she could not do it all and needed to concentrate on the most important aspects of the work. The boss hired a part-time temporary worker to relieve

Angie during the seasonal rush. She knew the work pressures lessened later in the year and Angie could handle the job by herself. Angie's boss had been through the seasonal cycle, Angie had not. If she had not asked for help she would not have gotten it.

Do not ask the boss for help when:

√ it is mindless work anyone can do,

√ help is obviously not needed (this annoys rather than flatters the boss),

√ the employee is trying to get out of doing a job, and

√ the employee has the authority to delegate the work to someone else.

Ask the boss for help when:

√ it is needed,

√ the boss can help get the project off the ground,

√ it is known that the boss has more experience in an area and the employees know their performance will be better with the boss's guidance,

√ there are problems with policies and procedures,

√ the work schedule is such that the employees need help setting priorities,

√ the task involves several departments,

√ the employees do not know how to get started and need an outline of the best way to proceed,

√ it is a precarious situation because of who or what is involved,

√ there might be disturbing complications,

√ the employees are concerned they might do something stupid,

√ the employees are unsure about the correct course of action,

√ the employees know it is something the boss enjoys and wants to do,

√ the boss tells the employees he or she wants to be involved,

√ a group of employees cannot work out who does what,

√ everybody has a different understanding of what has to be done.

What bosses are not up on they will be down on. They do not appreciate getting news about their department from someone else, even if it is good news. Unless it is routine work and checking with the boss makes employees look like they cannot do what they were hired to do, bosses want to know what is going on in their arena of operation and they do not feel they should have to play detective to find out.

Check with the new boss before proceeding when:

√ it is a situation the employees do not usually handle,

√ the person the employees are dealing with is likely to make trouble,

√ employees have innovative ideas,

√ employees decide to do a routine task in a new way,

√ employees feel they are in over their heads,

√ it involves a commitment of time, people, and money that goes beyond the employee's authority,

√ there is any doubt regarding procedure,

√ the bosses are not clear about what the employees are doing or why they are doing it,

√ it is a job the new boss knows more about than the employees do and they have reason to believe the boss has definite opinions on how the job should be done, and

√ someone else is going to tell the boss about the employees' projects.

Nicole did not like talking with new people and particularly wanted to avoid people in authority. So when a man approached her desk and demanded payment for a bill he presented, she took money from the petty cash fund and paid him. Months later the auditor discovered payment was made for services not provided. The boss took Nicole to task for not being more thorough. Nicole lost her responsibility for the discretionary fund.

Matthew worked with the building inspectors before, but did not know how the new boss wanted to deal with their visit. He checked with the boss and learned she wanted to meet and accompany them. She was new to the city and thought this a good way to acquaint herself with the procedure. She asked Matthew to come along and function as he usually did. She wanted orientation for herself. Even though the inspection was routine, Matthew did the right thing when he checked it out with his new boss.

Work is a cooperative effort. Employees do not like receiving orders or demands from their bosses. They are there to do the job and know their boss has a right to tell them what to do, but they prefer to be asked rather than ordered. Knowing that the boss's request does not really give them a choice does not change the preference. Employees find it easier to cooperate when they are treated with courtesy and respect. Bosses feel the same way. They do not want the employees to tell them that they must do a particular thing. Employees should treat their bosses with the same respect and courtesy they want for themselves. They propose a plan, present fact-based arguments, make comparisons, speak of the common good, and explain the advantages to the company, selling the idea to the bosses in a way that makes it sound agreeable and too good to pass up.

Employees who want something for themselves, such as paid training or an all-expense-paid trip to attend a conference, request the opportunities and explain what the company has traditionally done in the past. They include the benefits to the company such as better trained employees, knowledge brought back to the rest of the workers, and how they can organize their work to make the absences possible. The costs, the time away, and how the employees' work will be completed are all part of a complete report that gives the bosses enough information to make a decision. If the material is also in writing and left with the bosses, they have the data they need to reach a decision.

If employees want to change a procedure that would result in increased and better customer service, a cost-benefit plan helps the boss make a favorable decision. The boss wants to know what any change costs in money, time, and personnel, why the change is needed, and what the short- and long-term consequences might be. A proposal, such as an improved service plan, may legitimately contain an enumeration of the intangible values—for example, fewer complaints, happier customers, good public relations, improved reputation, repeat business, and more word-of-mouth referrals.

For employees concerned about working with old machinery that is hard to operate, breaks down, or is in some way dangerous, find it advisable to start with a cost-benefit report. The report should include the human factor of not being able to do a job that allows the employees to be proud of their work, the frustration of frequent down-time because of disabled equipment, and the liability issues related to unsafe machinery. Comparing the company's equipment with another company's and detailing their experience with the more dependable and safe machinery is an additional selling point.

The new boss scheduled Alice to work overtime to complete a rush job. Alice was looking forward to a special outing with her friends. She demanded the that boss assign the overtime to someone else. The boss responded to Alice's surliness by ordering her to work. Then Alice appealed to the boss, explaining her plans. The boss understood and requested that another employee stay and do the extra work.

Check it out with the new boss by keeping the following in mind:

1. The boss wants to hear about the employee's work from the employee and not from someone else.

2. The boss wants to be kept up-to-date on new and old projects.

3. The boss wants to get progress reports that are inclusive and contain both the good and the bad news.

4. The boss cannot feel positive about the employee's efforts if he or she is not made aware of what is happening.

5. The boss wants to know about anything out of the ordinary.

6. The boss wants to hear as soon as possible afterwards if the situation is such that he or she cannot be told beforehand.

7. The boss likes requests, not demands.

8. The boss responds to facts, requests, proposals, comparisons, appeals to the common good, information, reasons, and the prospect of additional dividends, but wants concerns addressed as well.

TACTIC # 32: COMMUNICATE WITH THE NEW MANAGER

Bert worked long enough to notice that the only time most employees got to see the boss was when they did something wrong. If it was this way for him and his coworkers, he reasoned, it was the same for his boss. Just because he did not hear kind words, he would not deprive his boss of praise and recognition. He resolved to let his boss know when the boss did well.

Employees are in a position to influence the boss. Conversations about work lead easily to opportunities for the employees to recognize the boss's contributions. There is no reason to be shy about expressing appreciation if the boss does something the employees like, or about giving commendations if the boss performs in ways that are remarkable or impressive.

When employees help the boss feel good the boss feels good about them.

Tanya was reticent and did not reach out to people. She could not think of anything to say. Although she appeared aloof, she was, in fact, terrified and tongue-tied. The idea of a new boss upset her as she knew she would get nervous and not be able to get her words out when the boss was around. So she rehearsed. She prepared for the day she would meet him. She knew what she would like to hear, so that is the message she prepared for her new boss. She offered him her support.

Letting bosses know they are welcome and the employees are happy to meet them is common courtesy and the kind of thing anyone would say to a newcomer. Exhibiting good manners is an engaging way to be friendly and considerate and help the boss feel comfortable in the new job. Employees reassure the new managers by letting the managers know they understand change is needed and they are prepared to work with them. Also, bosses are relieved and find it helpful to know what is going right so they can concentrate, instead, on fixing what is wrong. Loyalty to the company and acceptance of the change-over is demonstrated by offers of assistance and truthful reports about the work situation.

Terry could not resist people with power. He stuck to them like static cling. When the new boss took over he told her how much he welcomed her and how eagerly everyone awaited her arrival. So far so good, but he went on to tell her how awful everything was prior to her assumption of the position and how her arrival perked up all the employees. He complimented her on her appearance and behavior until she was ready to yell, "YUCK!" and run. Terry was a pest.

Crystal also welcomed her new boss but appeared more sincere. She acknowledged that the upheaval was difficult, but staff members were ready to settle down and get to work. She indicated they were good workers and would do a good job. The boss felt Crystal was ready to help and he was appreciative.

Reassure the new administrator in the following ways:
- √ offer cooperation,
- √ give support,
- √ explain what the employees have to offer,
- √ let the boss know the employees accept the fact that there will be changes,
- √ express confidence that the changes will be for the better,
- √ tell the boss what is going well,
- √ suggest ways the employees can help, and
- √ offer to work with the boss.

Reassurance helps because:
- √ employees are accepted as team members;
- √ there is less pressure on employees to prove themselves;
- √ the boss can relax;
- √ the boss is less suspicious and defensive;
- √ there may be fewer changes because the boss can take time to recognize what is working well;
- √ good work can continue;
- √ the boss can address what needs to be done;
- √ the employees create good will; and
- √ the employees feel good about taking positive actions.

Reassurance is a positive approach and new managers are drawn to positives. Expressing differences and helping the new bosses by providing the benefit of the employees' experience is one thing; criticism, even if it is intended as constructive, is another. There are not many people who want to be told anything for their own good, nor do they value constructive criticism (DeJonge, 1994). The usual response to criticism is defensiveness and determination to prove the other person wrong. New bosses, who are sensitive about their positions and want to prove themselves, do not want to listen to employees telling them what to do. They may proceed with a bad idea just because it was criticized. This is not to say that employees need to withhold knowledge and information. But telling the bosses what they need to know can be done in a positive, rather than negative way.

It is negative to attack and positive to show interest. You "did," "should," "never," or "always," sounds accusatory, while I "wonder," "worry," "think," "feel," sounds like the employees want to learn more. Employees who offer or ask for information sound involved, interested, and part of the project. They are enlarging the general pool of knowledge rather than attacking the boss for the limitation of his or her knowledge.

Vernon listened to his new boss's plan to move the office to another part of town, then spouted, "Don't you know the building we are in is owned by the chairman of the board, we have enough stationery to last two more years, and many of our customers live and work in this area?" He criticized the boss because he thought the boss had not considered all the exigencies of the move. Vernon had some good points, but the way he spoke made the boss determined to knock them down one by one. The chairman of the board was about to retire, the paper could be recycled, a move would keep the old and bring in new customers. The boss had several more reasons for the move that Vernon would have heard had he given his boss a chance to present his rationale. If he had listened all the way through he might have asked his questions or made his point by saying, "Will the move cause any problems with the landlord?" or "When will the move take place?" or "Will we continue to be accessible to our customers?"

Yvonne was showing off when she told the boss his actions were not thought through. She was quick to tell him about his mistakes, unpopular decisions, and less than perfect results. She thought the boss would be impressed with her knowledge and discernment. Yvonne forgot that the boss was human and that bosses have feelings, too. The boss's feeling was that Yvonne spent her time looking for missteps. Yvonne thought of herself as a trouble-shooter. The boss saw her as a trouble-maker.

Criticism, even if intended as constructive, is rarely well received:

- Speak up when something is seriously wrong, but use tact.
- Use the word "I" to express concerns and observations. The word "you" makes people defensive.
- Enlarge on the boss's knowledge instead of knocking the boss's ideas and plans.

Bosses infrequently get feedback from the employees they supervise. One reason is because they do not ask. The Hays Group, a consulting firm, found that 28 percent of 1,405 companies they studied never conducted an employee survey. Forty-four percent of the 28 percent of the companies that did not survey their employees were run by managers who did not want to ask or did not want to respond to employee concerns. Those companies preferred to think that their employees were content or they did not want to be bothered with employees' complaints (Cunniff, 1993).

Although bosses need to hear from their employees and, generally speaking, want feedback, they do not want constant challenges and criticisms. If they only hear complaints they tend to distance themselves so they cannot hear from the employees. Both inexperienced and experienced bosses do this. The inexperienced feel more secure with a buffer zone and the experienced probably tried listening to employees, got tired of the complaints, and decided to never do it again. This is understandable because people are attracted to pleasure and try to avoid pain. It happens to everyone, including presidents of the United States. They start out the term wanting to communicate with the people because they sincerely want to be responsive and announce they will be available to the press. They hold several press conferences, field complaints, concerns, and challenges, and soon find themselves too busy to have press conferences, their security too threatened for them to move among the people, and their comfort level enhanced by listening to official advisors for feedback and information. These advisors temper their criticisms and include positive feedback. This is much more palatable than the misery of hearing from the press about all that is going wrong. If people are rewarded for their actions, they are more likely to repeat them. If they are punished, they stop those behaviors that bring offensive results. This is behavior modification.

Bosses, like everybody else, are enticed by praise and approval. If what the bosses do is good and it works, they like to have their good work acknowledged. Staff members who give the boss credit and voice their accord should not be surprised to discover that the boss arranges for more occasions to talk with them. Employees who are truthful, but have a talent for reporting good news, get more audiences with the boss and also have more opportunities to give honest feedback that includes reports on problems.

Bosses are more likely to continue actions that bring compliments, praise, and compliance, leaving them less inclined to pursue unpopular pursuits. In other words, employees are more likely to get what they want if they praise what they like and ignore what they do not like.

In fact, people, including bosses, are insatiable when it comes to hearing positive comments. Mike Weingart of the Houston Business Journal reports a Chicago department store sells talking teddy bears as an answer to that need. They say, "You're a born leader," "You're a winner." Employees are not talking teddy bears, but they can give good news and compliments when appropriate.

Todd, along with most of the employees, felt that the personnel policies the new boss wrote were too restrictive. He and other staff members did acknowledge however, that there was a need for codified, uniform, and written policies. Previously, no one knew what benefits were available, what procedures needed to be followed to take time off, file grievances, apply for promotions, or quit the job. It was decided by whim and mood. Some employees had many privileges while others could not get paid time off when they were sick. Most every worker felt insecure. So Todd told the boss how much they appreciated his plan to formulate the personnel policies. He did not say they liked the policies. He said the staff members were eager to see the written policies. The new boss liked hearing that the employees were in agreement with him. As a result of this approval he asked the employees to appoint a committee to work with him. This gave them the opening they needed to feed in their ideas, compare their policies with those of other companies, and work out a mutually agreed upon set of standards.

Ava believed in letting the boss know when he did well. The problem was Ava seldom noticed that the boss did anything she liked. When she did find something praiseworthy she never failed to add a "but" and state what she did not like in the same sentence. The boss learned that Ava's praise was always followed by criticism. As a result the boss came to dread Ava's acclaim.

Praise the boss's good work and effective ideas keeping the following in mind:

- Bosses do not get a lot of good news and personal kudos.
- The boss would rather hear what he or she does right than what he or she does wrong.
- Bosses are drawn to employees who bring them pleasure through praise.
- When bosses get positive reinforcement they tend to continue in the direction that brought them praise.

Both employees and bosses need support through critical times. A change in management is a critical time for employees and for the new bosses. Bosses and employees need someone to talk with, to give them information, to tell them the truth, to be on their side, to keep them out of trouble, to help them with the company protocol, and to listen to ideas.

Because of the nature of their relationship, employees and bosses cannot always depend on each other for support, but employees, if they choose, can be supportive people for their bosses. Being a supportive person is not the same thing as being a "yes" person. Supportive people are available, helpful, understanding, and attentive. They interpret, clarify, explain, warn, question, enlarge, and suggest. They do not necessarily agree or flatter. They do not help others, including the boss, at their own expense. Supportive people help others, including the boss, because they gain something for themselves in the process. That is not selfish and self-centered. That is sensible. It is called altruistic egoism (Selye, 1976).

The difference between supporting the boss and sacrificing for the boss is easy to determine if employees pay attention to what they are doing to themselves. Employees who decide to be supportive are never obliged to go against their own values, put their own lives on hold, get nothing in return, hate themselves for their behaviors, lose their self-respect, or get into trouble in other areas of their lives in order to support their bosses. They support their bosses because of what they get in return, because they want to be helpful and make the transition as smooth as possible for everyone concerned, and because it is a friendly thing to do.

Self-sacrificing behavior is not required nor is it recommended. Not every boss expects, wants, or takes advantage of employees who cannot or do not draw the line between support and over-involvement; most would not want to, and none should be allowed to. Employees are not on the job to make everyone else happy, fix every troubled employee or situation, or ruin their own lives in order to help. There are boundaries in the worker-boss relationship that need to be respected and kept. The employee-employer relationship is a work relationship, and over-stepping those boundaries is counter-productive. When there is a danger signal that indicates the boss and the employee are getting trapped in an unhealthy relationship, the employee needs to take stock of what is happening and retreat. The signs to look for are the following:

- The employee thinks no one understands the boss as well as he or she does.
- The employee thinks the boss's needs are more important than the employee's needs.
- The employee neglects family, friends, and his or her own interests to take care of work and the boss's needs.
- The employee develops an inflated idea of the importance of his or her boss and the boss's work.
- The employee starts getting questions from friends, family members, and coworkers about his or her relationship with his or her boss.
- The employee finds him or herself unhappy when not working with his or her boss. Nothing else gives the employee the same excitement and satisfaction.
- The employee no longer notices if the boss is right or wrong, moral or immoral, legal or illegal. Support is given to the boss no matter what the boss does.

Valencia knew she was not indispensable, so she aimed to appear necessary. She decided the best way to do that was to give support to her new boss. If the boss relied on her, she calculated, her job would be secure. She made herself available. She listened. She flattered. She stuck with him, neglecting her own job responsibilities. She ignored the office gossip, the concern of her friends, and got more and more involved. She told herself it was all part of her job. Even when their togetherness led to sexual involvement and the dereliction of her responsibilities to her own family, she was not alert to the danger. He needed her. She went blindly on, telling herself she was being supportive. When the boss's wife became aware of the situation, ultimatums were stated. Guess who lost her job? Valencia needed support, but did not get it from her boss, her friends, or her family. She learned that support does not mean self neglect.

Brandon did not like changes in management, but he understood that changes take place. He also was wise enough to know the new boss was not coming to work just to pick on him. He knew he needed support throughout the changes and felt his new boss could use all the help she could get, too. To this end he was friendly and welcoming, but businesslike. He did not intrude, but let her know what was going on in an effort to keep her from doing unnecessary work and getting into trouble overriding well-thought-out procedures. He listened, explained, clarified, and told her when she did well. Their relationship was close, confined to work, and mutually rewarding.

Bosses need support too, and it is good to keep in mind the following:

1. It is supportive to listen, provide information, and give straight answers to questions.
2. Supportive people are available, helpful, and understanding.
3. Support is providing interpretations, clarifications, explanations, warnings, and suggestions.

CHAPTER EIGHT REVIEW

1. Does the boss know that the employees do not have designs on the boss's job?
2. Do employees enlist the boss's help when it is needed?
3. Does the boss know what work assignments are getting the employees' attention?
4. Do employees explain rather than make demands when they want something from the boss?
5. Do the bosses know they have the employees' cooperation and support?
6. Do the employees give negative information in tactful ways that do not threaten or accuse?
7. Do the employees give the bosses positive reinforcement when the bosses take action that fosters a good working environment?

CHAPTER 9

WORK WITH THE CHANGES

Arthur was isolated in his misery. He saw no reason to discuss his work problems if he could not come up with a plan to solve them. Since he saw no way out, his withdrawal continued. He brushed off concerns, suggestions, and offers of help, all of which he needed.

Life is more than the job. Life requires contacts with many people, inside and outside the workplace. Change is a challenge and causes chaotic thoughts and feelings. During such times, it is beneficial to inventory available resources and know that there are many possibilities for work and play.

TACTIC # 33: KEEP OUTSIDE CONTACTS

Caroline's energy went into her job. She had a new boss and changes happened faster than she could adjust to them. She did not see the changes as necessary, fought them, and built up a great deal of stress and fatigue. She spent her time off from work resting in bed. She cut herself off from everything but her work life and was not finding satisfaction in that.

When stress and torment are experienced in one endeavor, it is all the more essential for one to feel success and nurturing in other pursuits. If feelings of inadequacy prevail in the work area, other areas of life become crucial to self-worth. The significance of home, health, leisure, and relationships are amplified as they are necessary anchors to remind employees that work is only one element of life. Although work is a substantial segment of a person's life, it is not all there is.

People's distress in one portion of life is often so consuming they let it overflow into all areas of life. It is not unusual for people with pervasive work worries to compound their work problems by withdrawing from the very things that help them get through the bad times and continue to enjoy what is going well. Pessimists allow problems from work to invade every part of their existence. Optimists do "not let one setback contaminate" (Eberlin, 1997: 26) their whole life. They remind themselves, for example, that although the job is not going well, "My husband and I are still close and I find time to run at least a mile every day."

It is not uncommon for people to define themselves by what they do. When work is not going well, their life is not going well. Although it is hard to find pleasure when the mood is downcast, it is nevertheless essential to self-management and self-confidence.

Continued contacts with professional organizations that put employees in touch with others in their field are constructive. The usual interactions with coworkers or workers from other businesses, such as participating in team sports, meeting at after-work hangouts, attending inter-company meetings, and going to regular business lunches do the employees good. Employees will note that their business acquaintances treat them with the same regard as ever and they function as well as before. If the word is out that the employee is in trouble, one way of dispelling this talk is to be seen having a good time and appearing as relaxed and confidant as ever.

Employees' satisfaction in their roles as spouse, relative, parent, neighbor, friend, hobbyist, and player enhances self-esteem and morale. They see themselves as multi-dimensional people.

Employees who keep up their social and leisure activity routines feel structure and solidarity in their lives. That is comforting in difficult times. Choir rehearsal, outings to the movies, card games with friends, sky-diving practice, and any and all other commitments help employees feel valuable and wanted. If the good feelings do not come naturally, there is nothing wrong with faking it until a more positive disposition catches up.

If family members pick a crucial time to have their own crises, troubled employees should get involved and offer help. If there are projects that can be started or completed, now is the perfect time to do the job and feel the sense of accomplishment. Getting involved, making contributions, and nurturing a sense of belonging returns a feeling of normalcy to disrupted lives. Giving to needy people or causes that have urgent problems helps put personal predicaments in perspective.

Tom cut himself off from his friends because he was tired of hearing them talk about their jobs. Because of the change in management, his work life was so uncertain he could not bear to talk about it. He did not want to hear about his friends' complaints and competitions at work. He did the same with business associates and quit going for his workouts at the health club because he could not concentrate on what he was doing. His family could not get him involved in anything because he said he had things on his mind. He ended up with a lot of time to worry and with a feeling that nothing was going right in his world.

The reorganization of Kathy's workplace came on the heels of a painful divorce. She felt her life was the pits, but decided to concentrate on the aspects that were going well. She joined a parents-without-partners group so she could help others adjust to life without a mate. She also used this group to answer some of her social needs. She gave more time to her children, involving them in learning experiences, and participated in activities they could do together. Most of all, she kept up contacts with old friends who had seen her through her divorce and continued to stand by her during her work problems. Her interests kept her occupied and buoyed. She had her job stress, but did well in other areas of her life, and she knew it.

Steps to keeping up contacts outside of work include the following:

1. Recognize the job is only one aspect of a balanced life.
2. Keep up business contacts.
3. Do more, instead of less, with friends, family, and hobbies.
4. Keep up a normal life routine.
5. Get involved in an organization that needs and uses help.

TACTIC # 34: LOOK FOR OPTIONS

Since Jake decided to stay with the job, he considered the matter a closed issue. He shut his mind to further training and was not open to other career possibilities. He would not consider working anywhere else.

There is no reason to put on blinders. The more options people have or can develop, the more secure they are. Keeping a job out of desperation is negative; keeping the job because of preference is positive.

Explore all options, including those that can be developed and some that may not be immediately apparent. Search for hidden or long lost desires.

MONEY: Is another family member able to earn enough money for all family members so there is time to find something else? Are there savings?

SKILLS: Are job skills transferable? Is this an opportunity to go to school or open a business?

LOCATION: Is this the time to live in a warmer or colder climate, closer to relatives, in a more cosmopolitan area, or where hobbies such as boating, mountain climbing, or gardening can be pursued?

BENEFITS: What does the company offer in the way of benefits? Is early retirement, career counseling, a sabbatical, specialized training or retraining, or a transfer an interesting possibility?

OTHER OPPORTUNITIES: What is available locally? Can employment agencies or professional search companies help?

CONTACTS: Make use of business and social contacts. Talk to people. Let them know what is wanted and ask them who they know who can help.

Even though employees are secure in their decision to stay with the job, having other options enhances that security. In the United States, one out of six workers changes jobs every year. Obviously many workers exercise their options (Feinsilber & Mead, 1980).

Liz was overwhelmed at the idea she might have to look for another job. She had worked in her position for 20 years. She felt unqualified for anything else. But her security was threatened because rumor had it that the new managers wanted to get rid of people who had been with the company a long time because of their accrued salary and benefits. If she lost her job, she felt, all was lost. Liz's friends had more confidence in her than she had in herself. They suggested she write out everything she did on her job. When she did this she discovered she had many transferable skills and could do any one of a number of other jobs. This helped her feel secure. She wanted to keep her job, but knew she had talent and ability to find other work if she were forced to relinquish her position.

Evan dreamed of getting an advanced degree, but never availed himself of his company's tuition reimbursement program because he did not want to work and go to school at the same time. With the advent of new management he vowed to sign up for school immediately, no matter how much extra work it required. He wanted to be prepared to go further within the company, or to find a job of his choice if, at some point, his boss decided he no longer wanted to keep him.

Keep options open by doing the following:

1. Be alert to all work options.
2. Be creative when considering other job possibilities.
3. Research what options the company offers its employees.
4. Talk to career counselors.
5. Research what is available in similar work situations.
6. Inventory job skills.
7. Join professional organizations.

TACTIC # 35: WELCOME NEW EMPLOYEES

Jill was a friendly person. As much as she resented the changes in her work environment, she could not bring herself to be mean to innocent people who were trying to do their jobs. She helped them feel welcome by giving them her personal attention.

The social aspects of the workplace are sometimes more appealing than the work. Work is wonderful when working relationships are good. When new workers are hired, the familiar balance changes. The new employees cannot take the place of the former coworkers who were known and valued. In some primitive place in the mind lurks the thought that if the newcomers leave, the old workers will return. Of course, this will not happen. New management has no intention of returning to the old, if, in fact, they even know what the old was. The new is here to stay and, in time, it becomes the old. Employees may as well welcome new employees and make new work friends. Feelings of loss persist, but the behavior does not have to reflect that loss. Feelings come unbidden, but behaviors can be controlled ("Grin and Bear It," 1994).

New employees identify with new management. They got hired because they appeared to have the same ideas and goals as the new boss. They expect to work in harmony with new management and with their new coworkers. Consequently, the workers who are carried over into new management have the job of working to fit in. So, welcome the new employees. The newcomers want help and the old workers can give it by introducing them to people, projects, policies, procedures, and priorities. One thing the new workers do not want to hear is how things used to be. They want to know how to work with the way the company is now.

Once old workers understand that the new workers are there to stay and it is not the new workers' fault the system changed, they will have an easier time accepting and working with them. It takes less energy to work along with the eager new hires than to work against them.

New workers have their own routines and opinions. This does not make them wrong. It only makes them different. Different approaches are inconsequential if the job gets done. Everybody does not have to be, in fact cannot be, alike. There is work for both the old and the new workers.

Most companies have some sort of social routine at lunch and during breaks. Include the new workers in the group and get to know them. It takes time to feel close to new people, but everybody was a new worker at one time. Good relationships develop if given a chance.

All the new workers will not get along with all the old workers. This is to be expected. Few people like everybody they work with, but they work with them anyway. Employees do not have the luxury of deciding who they will or will not work with. They have to work with whomever is there, but they do not have to include them in their personal lives.

Brady recognized he was acting the way his kids did when he and his wife divorced. The children did not accept the new stepparents. They did everything they could to drive them off in the hope their parents would get back together and they could have everything the way it was before the divorce. Brady saw himself doing the same thing with the new employees. He wanted to drive them off and get his old coworkers back. However, he developed this insight before he went too far. He was able to change his approach and help the new employees settle in. He found he could work with them and they with him. They were people like Brady, with hopes and needs, and a desire to do a good job.

Dawn's supervisor had been accused of insubordination and a refusal to cooperate, and he was fired. A new employee was hired in his place. Dawn was asked to help her get oriented, as the new boss did not know the procedures any better than did the new supervisor. Dawn was so angry she was unable to do it. She felt it was enough that she did her own job. She told her new supervisor she did not know the procedures. She grumbled to her coworkers that the new supervisor was incompetent. She would not adjust, resigned her position, and left the office in disarray. The old and new employees had to struggle to get the job done. Not only did she not welcome the new workers, she caused difficulties for her friends who stayed on the job.

Welcome the new employees for the following reasons:
1. Welcoming the new employees helps the old employees adjust to the changes.
2. If the old workers work well with the new employees, the new employees will gladly work with them.
3. New employees need help to understand and fit into the work environment.

4. Cooperating and collaborating get the job done.
5. To include the new employees in work-related activities.
6. To get to know the new employees and develop good working relationships with them.
7. No one can expect to like all their coworkers, but they can expect to work well with them.

TACTIC # 36: HELP SUBORDINATES

Gene had a new boss, but the people he supervised still had him. He saw it as his job to help them through the adjustment period. He knew he could make it easier for them.

Supervisors can make change easier or harder for those they supervise.

Supervisors make change harder in the following ways:

√ complaining to their staff members,

√ being irritable about the changes,

√ acting hopeless,

√ proclaiming doom,

√ refusing to work within the new guidelines,

√ telling their employees that everybody is fed up,

√ acting defeated,

√ threatening to quit the job,

√ telling their workers that no one in the company is secure,

√ making their staff members listen to the supervisor's personal distress,

√ ignoring new procedures,

√ saying there is no hope that it will ever work out.

√ being insubordinate, and

√ repeating gossip and rumors about new management.

Supervisors' adjustment problems are not the employees' problems. Employees are not obliged to get sick when the

supervisor gets sick or have financial problems when the boss
has financial problems. Neither should they have to condemn
new management because their boss does. Leadership is a
requisite of good supervision. Leadership sets the tone and
expectations. Employees are helped through change when their
supervisors help them feel secure. When the supervisor copes
well, the employees tend to cope well, too.

Supervisors make change easier by doing the following:

√ explaining all changes,

√ remaining positive about the possibilities,

√ keeping staff members informed,

√ listening to the workers' frustrations and trying to
dispel them,

√ being aware when the changes are not working and
taking responsibility for discussing the problems
with the boss,

√ helping employees feel secure,

√ removing as many stresses as possible,

√ letting the workers know that change can be
managed, and

√ staying on the job.

Supervisors do not have to sacrifice themselves for their
employees. In fact, they should take good care of themselves so
that they can take good care of the people they supervise. They
take good care of the employees by giving them support and
direction so they can manage changes as they occur (Tager, 1987).

Tracy felt threatened by the new boss and thought she
might lose her job. She felt she could not protect herself and
wondered how she could protect those she supervised. But
she was determined not to pass her anguish on to them. She
did this by concentrating on the work to be accomplished instead
of on the personality of her new boss. If the people in her
department were aware of what she was going through, they

did not show it. They tackled the job as it was outlined by her. They complained about some things and were happy about others. In other words, it was business as usual. Tracy felt good about handling things this way. It turned out to be the best thing she could have done. It gave the new boss confidence in her. His attitude toward her changed from his initial fears of what she would be, and her sense of security returned. Her employees were not unduly distressed about the changes and did not have to go through a readjustment when she changed her mind about the new boss.

Warren felt everybody who was not against the new boss was against him. He made his attitude clear to those he supervised. They were expected to report any horrifying news they could dig up. They worked hard at keeping Warren informed about the boss's ominous actions. Warren and his employees spent most of the working day plotting ways to keep from doing what the new boss wanted them to do. When Warren heard about a chance to transfer to a different department he jumped on it, leaving the employees in his department with a new supervisor hired by the boss he had so thoroughly lambasted. The new department boss had a difficult time getting the workers to settle down and work due to their recalcitrant and uncooperative attitudes. Several of them were given warnings that were placed in their personnel files. Some of them left. Warren caused undue stress, hindered the workers' adjustment, and brought on long-term friction. Long after he was happily settled in a new job, they were struggling with their adjustments.

Supervisors' responsibilities to subordinates are to do the following:

1. Give clear directives.
2. Provide a good working environment.
3. Make it possible for them to do the best job they can.
4. Protect them from the supervisor's personal bias regarding new management.

TACTIC # 37: SET AN EXAMPLE

Halsey, because of self-interest, went about his work and appeared to accept changes with equanimity. He was amazed when, because of his demeanor, he was seen as a leader in his workgroup. That was the last thing he ever thought he would be. It gave him a new self-image.

Every employee in every new management situation suffers stress. It is not the anguished employee's job to make the circumstances more tolerable, but if they do not do it, who will? And if they do not do it for anyone else, they can at least do it for themselves. In the process, they, like Halsey, manage to look as though they know what they are doing. They are setting a good example. When they appear confident, other employees feel more confident. When they are not worried, other workers do not worry as much. If they do not show signs of insecurity, coworkers notice and feel more secure.

Employees who are surviving, and surviving well, are a source of comfort and inspiration to their coworkers. People grow tired of apprehension and anxiety. They latch on to something that gives them encouragement and hope.

Employees can further calm the suffering by presenting reasonable, encouraging statements, such as, "They need us more than we need them," "Our product is not obsolete," "We are doing a good job," "The changes are taking place at the management level, not with us," "It would be too expensive to train others for what we are doing," "The new contract includes the same benefits and pay," or "Job descriptions haven't changed."

Employees who are coping well pass on valuable information by talking about their coping skills. They talk about enjoyment of their leisure activities and about what is really important in their lives, such as family or avocational projects. They lighten up the workplace with humor and organize get-togethers aimed at giving and receiving support. These employees recognize that if they cannot change the situation, they can change how they handle it (Benson, 1976).

One of the major problems in adjusting to new management is worrying by anticipation. If employees keep focused on the present and get through today satisfactorily, they develop a conviction that they can also get through tomorrow. And as the days go on, they find that life has settled down and everybody is back into a comfortable routine.

Employees who are at ease with the new boss remove a lot of stress from the workplace by demonstrating that the boss is an approachable human being. Communicating with the boss, getting needed support and direction, and integrating the new guidelines into the work tells coworkers that the boss is not the menace they imagined him or her to be.

Janet worked well with her boss. They communicated with each other and admired each other's work. Janet felt appreciated, as did her boss. As a consequence, it was hard for Janet to see her boss move on. She did not want a new boss, but she wanted to keep her job. She only knew one way to work with a boss and that was through mutual respect. She had a good experience with her supervisor before and expected to again. Because of this she did not join in when her coworkers expressed their fears about the new boss. She said the company hired good people before and she was going to assume they had done so again. She welcomed the new boss and worked with her as she had with her past supervisor. The other employees saw Janet doing well and, bolstered by her success, followed her example. False antagonisms could have built up, but did not, thanks to Janet's level-headedness and good example.

Darrell knew he was no match for the rumor mill. If he listened to the gloom and doom, he would never find the time or motivation to do his job. He vowed to ignore the laments. He would see how well he could manage his work in the face of changes and threats of changes. He found that he could in fact manage well. As his mood and his production picked up, his coworkers took notice and decided if he could do it, so could they. As everyone settled down to the job, both Darrell and his coworkers felt relief that the crisis was behind them.

One employee can be an example for other employees in the following ways:
1. By demonstrating that continuity is possible.
2. By keeping worries in control.
3. By speaking words of encouragement.
4. By modeling stress reduction behaviors.
5. By taking care of today.
6. By showing that it is possible to work with the new boss.

TACTIC # 38: EMPHASIZE THE JOB

Hillary's satisfaction with her job was related to the work itself. She found it interesting and challenging (Kerr, 1988). She wanted to keep her job and continued working away, not letting the annoyance of change bother her.

Sometimes workers forget why they report in at their place of work every day. It is to do their job and to get paid for it. By concentrating on this main point, employees can emphasize their job and stay on track. When they do their job and feel the satisfaction of a job well done, they are doing what they were hired to do and are earning their salary. The days pass in gratifying labor and the financial rewards keep coming.

When employees attend to their jobs, they notice their good work. They can acknowledge their own accomplishments, as well as the accomplishments of their coworkers.

The boss is irrelevant as long as the job is there and the employees continue to do it. Whether or not the boss is liked is of little consequence if the employees enjoy their work. Workers are not asked to approve or disapprove of the boss. As long as the boss does not impede them in their work or stop their pay, it does not matter what the boss does.

If Valerie had a hobby, complaining was it. If she felt good, she was sure it would not last because a disaster of some type was just around the corner. If it was sunny and mild, she complained because she was not out enjoying the weather. If she looked good and was complimented, she complained that no one had noticed her yesterday when she went to so much effort to make herself look better. She remained true to form when the new boss arrived, complaining that nothing was done correctly. Valerie's coworker, Ida, was so exasperated with Valerie it was all she could do to keep from getting into a verbal battle with her. But Ida was resolute about concentrating on her job. She was so positive that her performance would not be deterred by Valerie's bad attitude that she put more effort into her work than ever before. She found she not only could continue to do a good job, but with the extra push performed better than she thought she could. Her success was apparent to her coworkers, and even to Valerie. Most of her coworkers were motivated to try her technique and also succeeded in keeping their worries in check and felt satisfaction in their work. Valerie, however, complained that they were making her look bad.

Ken enjoyed his work and did not like having it disrupted by the changes imposed by new management. When he discovered that his irritation with them was carrying over into his work performance, he knew he had to do something about his attitude. He recognized that he always enjoyed his work and felt fulfilled when he did a good job, so he decided he was not going to let his anxiety about his new boss change that. He concentrated on his job and realized he could discharge his duties as well as ever.

When at work, concentrate on work by considering the following:

1. The job is there because work needs to be done.
2. Employees should take pride in a job well done.
3. Good work deserves praise.

IF IT IS TIME TO LEAVE

All the survival techniques in this book do not fit all situations. Employees can pick and choose, using those that suit their styles and circumstances. Using these approaches gives employees a sense of control over what is happening to them. They can influence themselves and others in their work environment. Employees who follow the suggestions in this book will find relief from stress as they use stress management techniques and work at living a balanced life in which work is only one part of who they are and what they do. They will take pride in their accomplishments and enhance their reputations. They will make sure they get good job recommendations and they may even keep their jobs.

Nevertheless, in spite of cooperative, confident, conciliatory, and competent efforts, employees may lose their jobs for reasons that have nothing to do with them. Their task is to remind themselves that they gave all they could and it is now important to change their focus to their future. People lose their jobs for many reasons that are beyond their control. Some of these reasons might include the following:

1. The company downsized.
2. The job was eliminated.
3. New management brought in their own people.
4. The employee's skills were no longer needed or were obsolete.
5. The boss did not look at what individual employees contributed.
6. The employee had the misfortune to remind the boss of someone he or she could not stand.
7. The boss's relative was hired.
8. The company needed the employee's salary to increase its cash flow.

When it is time to leave because the job is no longer available or the employee no longer wants to work for the company, he or she can leave in style, giving himself or herself every advantage in a search for other jobs and a continued career. He or she wants to get good recommendations, not burn bridges, and leave on a positive note.

1. Get recommendations in writing. When employees get their recommendations before they leave, they know what is said about them. Bosses who hand the recommendations to the employees are more likely to give good reports when they know the employees are going to read them.

2. Write resignation letters that enumerate contributions. The employee's resignation letter goes into his or her personnel file. The personnel file is handled by people who handle papers much more than they handle people. They may not know the employee about whom a prospective employer is asking. In fact, after a period of time, no one may recall the employee at all. The resignation letter that recounts the employee's positive history becomes the basis for the answer to the inquiry and makes a good impact on both old and new employers.

3. Be courteous and respectful about the departure. Employees never know when they will run into coworkers or old bosses. Good words from them may make a big difference in a person's career. The urge to be vengeful and lash out may be strong but will not accomplish anything. Leaving with a confident and professional attitude makes a good and lasting impression. Doing well is the best revenge.

4. Be useful right on through to the last day. Employees are paid to work as long as they are at work. They do not want to be remembered as people who goofed off or caused trouble in their last days at work. They want to be remembered as trustworthy and loyal employees who were going to something better.

Employees who move on to new jobs have the challenge of adjusting to changed circumstances and new management of their choice. The pointers in this book will benefit them as they find success in their new positions.

CHAPTER NINE REVIEW

1. Is a support system that the employees can trust available to them?
2. Are established employees accepting and working with the new employees?
3. Are the new hires included in work-related activities?
4. Are long-term employees cooperating and collaborating with the new employees to get their jobs done?
5. Are supervisors helping their staff members through the changes by making them feel productive and secure?
6. Are coworkers giving each other encouragement?
7. Are employees demonstrating that they can work with the new boss?
8. Do employees take pride in a job well done?
9. Are employees who leave making sure they leave on good terms and with good recommendations?

TAKE CARE OF SELF, JOB, BOSS, AND COWORKERS

Books, articles, and newspaper stories are replete with ways for managers to make change less painful and more effective for themselves and their employees. None of the authors claim that change is easy, but techniques suggested are designed to make change less traumatic for the employees. This is not altruism; it is because contented employees are more motivated and productive. For example, Ornstein & Sobel (1987) report that strong support from the boss is good for the employee's health. It prevents illness. This results in more profitable days at work.

Kanter (1990) relates the story of Western Airlines' merger with Delta Airlines. Delta's management was sensitive to Western Airlines employees' distress and acknowledged and encouraged them to mourn their losses. One of the Western executives eulogized the airline in a written testimonial that was sent to all employees. The manager said, "A final wish for the lives of us who mourn is to go on with joyful memories" (p. 84). A ceremony for 80 Western managers included writing out their fears related to the merger, burning them, and then donning caps and gowns to walk across a stage to receive a Doctorate in Merger Management degree and a graduation gift of the merged company's stock. Western workers were further helped to see value in their work and their company when Delta stressed its version of a "great future" by coining a slogan that verified Western's worth and contributions. The rallying cry was "The Best Get Better" (p. 85). Western managers continued to report to work, claiming it was business as usual. This was a reassuring manifestation of continuity. Delta quieted apprehensions by immediately establishing a pattern of "openness and communication" (p. 87). They sent concise, but complete, information to workplaces and employees' homes. They spelled out procedures for traveling and moving expense reimbursements, how job offers would be made, and gave "general information about the transition from Western's benefit programs to Delta's" (p. 86). Western offered the employees help with merger problems by providing counselors, rap sessions, pamphlets, educational aids, seminars, and videotapes. This well-planned merger worked, but was not devoid of unhappiness and feelings of disempowerment as Western employees were moved to other locations, demoted because of redundancy within the company, and subjected to new policies and procedures-including Delta's more rigid dress code.

Douglas McGregor, wrote about "The Human Side of Enterprise" as long ago as 1957 and "stressed man's potentials, emphasized man's growth, and elevated man's role in industrial society" (McGregor, 1966: xiv). Information about employee motivation has been available for decades. Management knows how to assist disaffected employees through change. They are aware of the stress of change and the problems of morale and performance that result. This does not mean they always follow recommended guidelines. And, even if they do, it is the employee's responsibility to take care of himself or herself.

SELF-CARE

In the 1997 movie, "Donnie Brasco," a downtrodden mid-level Mafia hit man expresses his concern about the elevation of a younger man he befriended to a job he thought was more appropriately his own. He recounts his long-term loyalty and how he followed orders without question or back-talk, and he wonders why he was passed over. He expresses his resentment and jealousy over his friend's appointment and his fear for his future because of new management. He talks about buying a big boat and going away. But he accedes to the changes mandated by the new boss because he is an ingrained part of the company. It is his life and he cannot imagine other options, except in pure fantasy. In his own way, he acknowledged, understood, and accepted his anger (Freeman, 1990) and made peace with the system, largely because when all was said and done, he had no intention of leaving it. The movie shows his continued dedication to his job.

Dr. Hugh Leavell (1995: D2) says the ability to let go is one of the "most useful, sanity-enhancing life skills." Whether it is hurt, anger, a situation, or a lost dream, at some point letting go becomes the wisest thing to do. Even good things come to an end, or change. He recommends turning away from thoughts of fear, regret, and longing by getting absorbed in new positive thoughts so there is no room for the old negative ones.

Everything is always changing. The present never lasts. Thomas F. Crum (1988: 153) points out that change "is not a philosophical choice. It is a survival choice. It is a choice for growth and flexibility." Shannon Brownlee (1997) contends that the human capacity for play is what keeps people flexible.

Without an appetite for fun, excitement, and variety, humans would not make adaptations to changed diets, jobs, mates, political systems, social conventions, and climate. One way for employees to take care of themselves is to make sure there are plenty of light-hearted moments in their lives and that they make time for the enjoyment of good things. Consider the wisdom in the old saying, "All work and no play makes Jack a dull boy."

The Ford Foundation researchers went to the "Desktop Color Printer group at Xerox and got its management and workers to accept the idea that restructuring the workplace with family life in mind would benefit everyone, both workers and companies" (Bases, 1997: A7). As much as this goes against the efficiencies of cutting costs and reducing staff, it worked. In May 1994, a successful product was produced. People were not hurt in the process and quality was not undermined. Companies can consider the employee's needs for play, support, and health and continue to produce and make money, but they cannot stop change. The employers can only do so much. It is the employee's responsibility to take good care of himself or herself and his or her life. Besides making sure they are getting what they want and need in life, employees are challenged to constantly upgrade their abilities and develop opportunities and options for themselves.

Hope is an important element for getting people through tough times and providing inspiration during good times, but hope has to be acted on if achievement is the desired result. According to Dr. David Viscott (1996), relying on hope alone stunts growth. Instead of hoping, he says, people should believe in themselves and take action.

Taking action involves recognizing and updating skills. This gives employees freedom to make choices regarding jobs and job changes. When they know they are free to pursue other interests, they are also free to stay through a difficult change-over. This attitude makes it easier to tolerate change. Because employees develop options, they can make the choice that is best for them and either stay or leave. Up-to-date employees avoid obsolescence, stay current, go back to school, learn new technology, stay in touch with changes in whatever field they are working, and demonstrate ability to adapt to change.

Receiving support through difficult times makes everything more tolerable. Support from family and friends is crucial, but hard for those close to the troubled employees because they are also upset, and get impatient and struggle with their own feelings. Accordingly, employees who want to take time off work or pursue other goals should be prepared to give as well as get. If they expect support from family and friends, they need to give support in return. They may find it necessary to find support from other sources in order to give their families a break. They can do this by getting involved in activities and organizations, both social and professional, and surfing the Internet. There are Internet job hunt sites, support groups, forums, and real time chat rooms (Jandt & Nemnich, 1997). Support is available from many sources. Many companies have employee assistance programs that have been established to meet the workers' crises and make referrals to local resources. Workers with problems owe it to themselves to find the support they need for as long as they need it. Employees who take care of themselves are taking care of their most important asset.

JOB-CARE

No one but the employees can take care of their jobs. No one can make employees do the job at the right time and in the right way. Employees have control over themselves and their work. Bosses can set the tone and optimize working conditions, but they cannot motivate employees. Employees motivate themselves. One way they do this is through self-talk. People keep up a constant mental dialogue that is frequently negative, often meandering, and usually forgotten. During stressful times, self-talk is fretful. It does not have to be that way. Humans can program their thoughts and make them constructive. Self-talk, when feeling insecure about the developments at work, can be tailored to meet the needs of the situation. Instead of concentrating on all the distressing events and changes, employees can change their thoughts to what they can do, have done, and what they have to offer. There is no logical reason to focus on what is wrong, what can go wrong, and what is beyond the employee's control. Workers can create a positive vision of what the job can be under new management and continue to give themselves encouragement. Dr. Shad Helmstetter in "The Self-Talk Solution" (1988: 183-204) dedicates a whole chapter to self-talk for job, career, and management. All of his self-talk statements are positive, encouraging, and achievement oriented. Every employee can make up their own customized self-talk and suggest to themselves that they are good workers, valuable employees, people who can handle whatever career problems present themselves, and prevail over adversity.

Sharing the vision consolidates good self-talk (Morgan, 1988). A subliminal understanding of the constancy of change is useful, but a clear verbal statement to a friend or relative regarding change and adaptation to change makes it truth. What employees plan to do to take advantage of change is better conceptualized when spoken. When people hear themselves speak they enlarge on their own understanding.

Most people work a regular 40-hour week with two weeks off for vacation and a few days for sick leave. This means they spend more time at work than they do at anything else, except sleeping. It is doubtful anyone eats, plays, or even watches television more than eight hours a day. Consequently, workers may as well enjoy their work. Anything that takes that much time and energy should contribute to a good life in more ways than financially. Enjoying the rewards of work is fine, but enjoying work itself adds quality and richness to the lives of workers. If the job is dismal, there are two choices. Employees can find a job they like better or they can change their attitudes. Allen W. Smith (1997) tells the story of a woman who hated her job so much she gave notice that she would leave in six weeks. So relieved was she with this action that she became downright cheerful. Her manner had a good effect on her coworkers who were drawn to her happy demeanor and became more content themselves. When her last day dawned, she did not want to leave because she was having such a good time. She delayed her departure and worked at her job for several more years, discovering it was not the job that was miserable, it was her. With her new attitude she was a happy employee.

Attitude also is the impetus for making the job better. There is more than one way to do almost everything (Emmerling, 1991). There may always loom an even better way. Employees who challenge themselves to analyze the job to find ways to make it more fun, more efficient, and more productive make their jobs more interesting. They may also make their jobs better or create new and improved jobs for themselves.

Being liked by others is more important to some individuals than to others. However, that is always important for people who want to keep their jobs. The more an employee is liked, the greater the likelihood he or she will keep his or her job. "People who keep their jobs generally work efficiently and are well liked" (Hales & Hales, 1997). People who know how to get along with others and adjust to the new system and new politics have a better chance of keeping their jobs than do people who are skilled, but have rotten personalities and do not fit in. "Seventy-five percent, the overwhelming majority, failed because they were unskilled in office politics" (Kennedy, 1980: 27). They did not get along with the boss, their peers, or go along with the organization problems. Some people could not get along with anybody.

Pleasing others on the job is essential, but so is pleasing the customer. Even if the priority of the company is not pleasing customers, the managers start to notice when they get complaints. Any organization that does not respond to their customer's need is an organization in trouble. Employees help themselves and their company by doing a good job and showing concern for the final product. When the product is not right, constant problems result (Crosby, 1984). Employees do not want those problems to come back on them.

Get along, fit in, do the job right, and interface with as many other people, organizations, departments, and teams as possible (Bridges, 1988). This is working on the growing edge. Employees who interface are learning and establishing relationships that insure survival "in a world of increasing interdependency" (Bridges, 1988: 165). In fact, as mentioned earlier: "The people who work along the interface between the organization and its external environment are the sources of all the information that is needed to survive in this rapidly changing world." The interfaces do not show up on organizational charts and the employees in these positions are often overworked. However, these are the employees who make themselves valuable because they are where the work most needs to be done. In addition, their work is loosely defined so they get to create their own place in the company, and they work outside their area of expertise. They diversify and become less vulnerable to dislocations, are more secure as their jobs are a composite of many things, and are less bored because they do not have routine jobs. In the meantime, employees profit from these "on the edge" jobs by keeping files on all achievements and contacts for use when they want to be considered for other jobs. Employers make good use of employees who are comfortable in work areas that go beyond their assigned jobs. Practice makes employees better at one job—learning new things makes employees suitable for many jobs (Gould, 1997). Employees who enhance their own abilities and design their own jobs end up managing their own careers.

BOSS-CARE

The very least employees can do is also the most consequential, and that is to show courtesy to the new boss. Etiquette in business is as important as etiquette anywhere (Half, 1990). Courtesy is acknowledging the boss's arrival, welcoming him or her, making introductions and offering to help. Employees do not make good first impressions when they ignore the boss or are rude. Employees who help their bosses get comfortable in their new setting are off to a good start. Bosses, like everyone else, gravitate to people who are pleasant.

A new boss was agitated to learn that an employee stayed home for three days to care for a sick family member. When the employee returned, the boss confronted her with a harsh reminder of her job responsibility and told her she would have to work out other arrangements for care should a similar situation occur. She graciously agreed and told him it would not happen again. That was not only courteous, it was smart. She reassured her boss that he did not have to worry about her and she was not going to take advantage of new management. She let him know that she would take care of her problems, and that she understood her duty to her job. She also knew this was not the time to ask for a raise or any special favors (Kiam, 1989).

In the long run, employees are noticed for their good work. In the short run, which is the crucial time for impressing the new manager, employees are noticed for how they dress, act, and get along with other staff members. Employees may have the good luck to be in the right place at the right time and make a favorable impression by also doing the right thing. But that is not something employees can count on, nor do they have to. Employees take charge of their boss's perception of them by making sure the boss sees them working, knows what they are working on, and understands how their work fits into the company's goals.

Relying on chance is not the way to get known by the new manager. Invite the boss along for lunch. Offer to help with the reorganization. Be nice to the boss's secretary, assistant, receptionist, and any people the boss brought along from the last job. Their reports will indicate if the employees were courteous and helpful or ill-mannered and unkind. Succeeding is the result of hard work, not luck (Half, 1990). Luck comes after employees work to prepare themselves to take advantage of any good luck that comes their way.

Bosses, especially new bosses, want to be kept informed (Norris, 1997). They know they do not know what is going on and appreciate all the help they can get. They do not want information given them in a condescending way, but in an informative manner that keeps them up-to-date and acknowledges their need to know. Employees who do this give the boss a vote of confidence. Employees who recognize that new managers, whether or not they are new as managers, suffer from the normal insecurity that comes with a new job (Littauer, 1984). Employees who help their bosses feel confident are looked on with favor. Who can dislike someone who makes them feel good about themselves?

Treating bosses as integral to the work environment means treating them with respect, courtesy, and consideration. Anybody who has been a boss or can put themselves in the boss's place understands their need to be included, informed, and appreciated. Since bosses are here to stay, employees may as well use them to further their effectiveness on their jobs.

COWORKER-CARE

Working with others is part of the joy of work and part of the frustration. Part of doing a good job and keeping it is getting along with all the people in the work environment.

Whenever there is a management change-over, coworkers are more important to each other and, at the same time, more aggravating. The employees who are supportive help each other adjust to change. Employees who agitate their coworkers make difficult times more stressful. The former cause positive emotions, the latter negative.

Anger is never in short supply when there is change or the threat of change. Employees who are angry can acknowledge it, but how they handle it determines how well they manage their emotions and how helpful they can be to their coworkers. Expressing anger is one choice, and not necessarily a bad one, if it is done discreetly, appropriately, and in the right place. Raging does not make anger less potent. It upsets everyone in the workplace and makes the anger worse. Carol Travis (1982: 143-144) writes, "The psychological rationales for ventilating anger do not stand up under experimental scrutiny. The weight of evidence indicates precisely the opposite: expressing anger makes you angrier, solidifies an angry attitude, and establishes a hostile habit." It is better to wait or engage in a distracting activity until the anger feels less intense and a logical plan for handling the situation is developed. Brooding, taking revenge, taking it out on someone else, and subterfuge are not recommended. Neither is it good to "let it all out." Coworkers don't want to hear it. Nobody wants to work in a place where people rant and rave whenever they feel like doing so (Rosellini & Worden, 1985). It is too hard on everyone. It is ruinous to relationships and to work reputations.

If there are disagreements with coworkers, it is better to set a time to hash it out rather than impulsively fight it out. When employees find out they are in the wrong, an apology does little harm to the pride and does a world of good for the relationship.

Conflict can be, but does not have to be, a major work stress (Calano & Salzman, 1988). When confronting conflict, employees can face the problem or look for someone to blame.

Trying to convince a coworker that he or she, not the other employee, is wrong is sure to fail and result in enmity. Attacking the problem and finding a solution results in a satisfactory solution. Coworkers remain allies.

Nobody is thrilled with criticism. If it must be given, give it in a way that allows the coworkers to discuss the topic and keep their self-respect. Check if the timing is right. If the coworker has just received bad news, is not feeling well, or was stuck on the expressway for an extra hour, postpone the criticism. If the employee doing the criticizing does not have time to stick around and discuss the problem, the timing is wrong (Simon, 1978). Criticizing and running is tempting, but unkind, unpopular, and ultimately unproductive.

"All organizations need teamwork, whether they are large or small, simple or complex" (Green, 1989: 181). Teams consist of one or more people of the same or different disciplines who work together to accomplish common objectives. Teams are temporary or permanent with supervision from one boss, or team members may report to different bosses. Team members have different personalities and specialties, but they all work with shared purpose. Good team members are competent in their field, able to communicate with all the team members, cooperative, can work for the benefit of the entire group, and are responsive to each team member's contribution. Good team members are not prima donnas, detail-oriented perfectionists, or back-stabbers. People who work well on teams worry less about individual recognition and more about the team's efforts toward the final result.

Working as a team member is advantageous to employees in that they have the opportunity to develop various skills, meet and work with many people, improve their ability to communicate with others, and acquire mutual trust. Employees also learn to work with the miscellaneous idiosyncrasies of their coworkers and grow in their ability to tolerate differences.

Being a team player does not necessarily mean the employees work with a set group of coworkers. It means that employees are able to work together companionably and in sync with the company's goals. Workers do not compete with each other. In-house competition depresses performance and ideas (Kanter, 1989).

Employees are responsible for good working relationships with their coworkers, but they are not responsible for their coworkers. Employees who welcome new workers are doing the right thing. But they are not obligated to let a needy new employee monopolize all their time to the exclusion of other friends at work. Nor should employees be responsible for a new worker's happiness outside the workplace. Good will is fine, caretaking is going too far.

Through it all, employees need a good sense of humor, the ability to tell a funny anecdote, and a willingness to chuckle at themselves. A good laugh is excellent self- and coworker-care.

Stress, after all, is less a result of the event itself, and more a result of the individual's perception of the event. As stressful as change is, it is more stressful when managed poorly. By taking care of themselves, their boss, their work, and their coworkers, employees will perform and prosper.

CHAPTER TEN REVIEW

1. Does the employee know how to handle anger, conflict, and criticism?
2. Can the employee let go of the past, accept the present, and move into the future?
3. Is the employee flexible and able to adapt to new situations?
4. Does the employee believe in her or himself?
5. Does the employee keep up contacts, interests, and abilities?
6. Is a positive mental dialogue an ongoing self-improvement project?
7. Has the employee found ways to make the job more interesting?
8. Does the employee know how to get along with others?
9. Is the employee courteous and thoughtful toward the boss and the coworkers?
10. Does the employee have the skills to work with a team of coworkers?
11. Does the employee evidence a good sense of humor?

REFERENCES

Amos, Wally. 1994. "Some Good Rules for Bad Times." *Parade Magazine*, May 22, p. 5.

Bases, Daniel J. 1997. "Human Factor Sometimes Missed in the Workplace." *The Tribune*, January 2, p. A7. Ft. Pierce, FL.

Benson, Herbert and Miriam Z. Klipper. 1976. *The Relaxation Response*. New York: Avon.

Bern, Paula. 1987. *How to Work for a Woman Boss: Even if You'd Rather Not*. New York: Dodd, Mead.

Bock, Doug, Tony Clark and Mike Cornett. 1973. *Is That You Out There? Exploring Authentic Communication*. Columbus, OH: Charles E. Merrill.

Bowes, Lee. 1987. *No One Need Apply: Getting and Keeping the Best Workers*. Boston, MA: Harvard Business School.

Bridges, William. 1988. "Making Change Work for You." pp. 161-181 in *Surviving Corporate Transition*. New York: Doubleday.

Boyd, L. M. 1966. "Curiosity Shop." *The Tribune*, October 28, p. D2. Ft. Pierce, FL.

Brophy, Beth. 1988. "Nice Guys (and Workshops) Finish First." *U. S. News & World Report*, August 22, p. 44.

Brothers, Joyce. 1978. *How to Get Whatever You Want Out of Life*. New York: Ballantine.

Brownlee, Shannon. 1997. "The Case for Frivolity." *U. S. News & World Report*, February 3, pp. 45-49.

Calano, Jimmy and Jeff Salzman. 1988. "Overcome Conflict and Come Out Ahead." pp. 177-185 in *Career Tracking: 28 Success Shortcuts to the Top*. Boulder, CO: CareerTrack.

Carnegie, Dale. 1936. *How to Win Friends and Influence People*. New York: Simon & Schuster.

_____. 1951. *How to Stop Worrying and Start Living*. New York: Simon & Schuster.

Carr, Clay. 1989. *The New Manager's Survival Manual: All the Skills You Need for Success*. New York: John Wiley & Sons.

Carr, Clay and Mary Fletcher. 1970. *The Manager's Troubleshooter: Pinpointing the Causes and Cures of 125 Supervisory Problems*. Englewood Cliffs, NY: Prentice Hall.

Chapman, Elwood N. 1982. *Supervisor's Survival Kit*. 3rd ed. Chicago: Science Research.

Coffin, Royce A. 1975. *The Communicator: How to Get Your Meanings and Messages Across in the Business and Social World*. New York: Barnes & Noble.

Crosby, Phillip B. 1984. *Quality Without Tears: The Art of Hassle-Free Management*. New York: McGraw-Hill.

Crum, Thomas F. 1988. *The Magic of Conflict*. New York: Touchstone.

Crutsinger, Martin. 1966. "Study: U.S. Wage Stagnation Getting Worse." *The Tribune*, September 1, p. A3. Ft. Pierce, FL.

Cunniff, John. 1993. "Do You Know What Your Workers Think? Employers Don't Want To." *The Tribune*, January 18, p. D4. Ft. Pierce, FL.

DeJonge, Joanne E. 1994. "Criticism Never Helps." *The Banner*, May, pp. 12-13.

Department of Commerce. 1996. *The National Data Book*. 116th ed. Washington, DC: U. S. Government Printing Office.

Donnelly, James H. 1992. *Close to the Customer: 25 Management Tips From the Other Side of the Counter.* Homewood, IL: Business One Irwin.

"Don't Hide From Change." 1992. *Working Smart*, June, p. 6.

Dyer, Wayne W. 1978. *Pulling Your Own Strings.* New York: Thomas Y. Crowell.

_____. 1980. *The Sky's the Limit.* New York: Pocket.

Eberlein, Tamara. 1997. "Are You an Optimist?" *Reader's Digest*, April, pp. 25-28.

Eigen, Barry. 1990. *Think Like a Boss and Get Ahead at Work: How it Really Works on the Inside.* New York: Carol Communications.

Emmerling, John. 1991. *It Only Takes One: How to Create the Right Idea-and Then Make it Happen.* New York: Simon & Schuster.

Estess, Patricia Schiff. 1966. "Preparing for a Layoff and Your Next Job." *Parenting*, November, p. 72.

Feinsilber, Mike and William B. Mead. 1980. *American Averages: Amazing Facts of Everyday Life.* Garden City, NY: Doubleday.

Freeman, Lucy. 1990. *Our Inner World of Rage.* New York: Continuum.

Garfield, Charles A. 1992. *Second to None: How Our Smartest Companies Put People First.* Homewood, IL: Business One Irwin.

Gerber, Jane Levenberg. 1997. "Been There, Done That, Now What? Becoming 'Unstuck' in Work with Family Systems." Paper presented on February 21 at a workshop of the National Association of Social Workers, Melbourne, FL.

Gould, Stephen Jay. 1997. "Strategies for Excellence." *Bottom Line Personal*, February 2, p. 9.

Green, Gordon W. 1989. *Getting Ahead at Work.* New York: Carol Communications.

"Grin and bear it." 1994. *The Tribune*, May 24, p. D1. Ft. Pierce, FL.

Hales, Dianne and Robert E. Hales. 1997. "Does Somebody Want Your Job?" *Parade Magazine*, March 16, pp. 14-19.

Half, Robert. 1990. "Etiquette." pp. 20-29 and "Forget Luck." pp. 45-52 in *How to Get a Better Job in This Crazy World*. New York: Crown.

Hampton, David R., Charles Edgar Summer and Ross A. Webber. 1987. *Organizational Behavior and the Practice of Management*. 5th ed. Glenview, IL: Scott, Foresman.

Helmstetter, Shad. 1988. "Self-Talk for Job, Career, and Management." pp. 183-204 in *The Self-Talk Solution*. New York: Pocket.

Horton, Thomas R. 1992. *The CEO Paradox: The Privilege and Accountability of Leadership*. New York: American Management Association.

Hughes, Marylou. 1993. *Quick fixes: 303 Ways to Help Yourself Before the Therapist Arrives*. New York: Crossroad.

Hyatt, Carole and Linda Gottlieb. 1987. *When Smart People Fail*. New York: Simon & Schuster.

Jandt, Fred E. and Mary B. Nemnich. 1997. *Using the Internet and the World Wide Web in Your Job Search*. Indianapolis, IN: JIST Works.

Kanter, Rosabeth Moss. 1989. *When Giants Learn to Dance*. New York: Touchstone.

Kennedy, Marilyn Moats. 1980. *Office Politics: Seizing Power, Wielding Clout*. Chicago: Follett.

Kiam, Victor. 1989. *Living to Win: Achieving Success in Life and Business*. New York: Harper & Row.

Latting, Jean Kantambu. 1992. "Giving Corrective Feedback: A Decisional Analysis." *Social Work* 37: 424-429.

Lawless, David J. 1972. *Effective Management: Social Psychological Approach*. Englewood Cliffs, NJ: Prentice Hall.

Leavell, Hugh. 1995. "There Comes a Time to Let Go." *Palm Beach Post*, August 4, p. D2. West Palm Beach, FL.

Littauer, Florence. 1984. *How to Get Along With Difficult People*. Eugene, OR: Harvest House.

Lorsch, Jay W., James P. Baughman, James Reece and Henry Mintzberg. 1978. *Understanding Management.* New York: Harper & Row.

McGarvey, Robert. 1990. "Talk Yourself Up." *USAir*, pp. 88-94.

McGregor, Douglas. 1966. *Leadership and Motivation.* Cambridge, MA: M.I.T.

McQuaig, Jack, Peter L. McQuaig and Donald H. McQuaig. 1981. *How to Interview and Hire Productive People.* New York: Frederick Fell.

Morgan, Gareth. 1988. "Sharing the Vision." pp. 46-53 in *Riding the Waves of Change.* San Francisco: Jossey-Bass.

Norris, Kenneth E. 1987. *Winning at Work: The Road to Career Success.* Blue Ridge Summit, PA: Tab.

Odom, Maida. 1993. "Kissing Up to Boss Has its Pluses." *The Tribune*, August 16, pp. D1, D3. Ft. Pierce, FL.

Ornstein, Robert and David Sobel. 1987. *The Healing Brain: Breakthrough Discoveries About How the Brain Keeps Us Healthy.* New York: Touchstone.

Patton, Bobby R. and Kim Giffin. 1981. *Interpersonal Communication in Action.* 3rd ed. New York: Harper & Row.

Peters, Tom. 1992. *Liberation Management* (Cassette Recording). CA: Excel.

Redford, S. R. 1978. *Jobmanship: How to Get Ahead by "Psyching Out" Your Boss and Co-workers.* New York: Macmillan.

Rogers, Carl R. 1973. "The Characteristics of a Helping Relationship." pp. 391-396. in *Readings in Managerial Psychology.* 2nd ed., edited by Harold J. Leavitt and Louis R. Pondy. Chicago: The University of Chicago.

Rosellini, Gayle and Worden, Mark. 1985. *Of Course You're Angry.* Center City, MN: Hazeldon.

Rubin, Theodore Isaac. 1969. *The Winner's Notebook.* New York: Pocket.

Ruch, Floyd Leon. 1958. *Psychology and Life.* 7th ed. Atlanta, GA: Scott, Foresman.

Selye, Hans. 1976. *The Stress of Life.* New York: McGraw-Hill.

Schoenberg, Robert J. 1978. *The Art of Being a Boss*. Philadelphia: J. B. Lippincott.

Simon, Herbert A. 1976. *Administrative Behavior: A Study of Decision-Making Processes in Administrative Organization*. 3rd ed. New York: Free Press.

Simon, Sidney B. 1978. *Negative Criticism*. Allen, TX: Argus Communications.

Smith, Allen W. 1996. "Discipline goes a long way." *The Tribune*, October 26, p. D1. Ft. Pierce, FL.

_____. 1997. "Enjoy work as much as leisure." *The Tribune*, March 19, pp. D1, D3. Ft. Pierce, FL.

Staff. 1997. 'Things that Help Us Deal with Stress and Help Us to Succeed!" *Various & Sundry Things*, February, p. 1.

Stephens, Lisa. 1991. *Willpower: Find the Strength*. New York: Prentice Hall.

Suriano, Robyn. 1994. "Pearl Clark a Jewel for HRS District." *The Tribune*, June 25, pp. B1, B3. Ft. Pierce, FL.

Tager, Mark J. 1987. "Job-Related Stress: The Manager's Role." *EAP Digest*, July/August, pp. 39-44.

Travis, Carol. 1982. *Anger: The Misunderstood Emotion*. New York: Touchstone.

Viscott, David. 1996. *Emotional Resilience*. New York: Harmony.

_____. 1977. *Risking*. New York: Pocket.

Waitley, Denis. 1980. *The Winner's Edge*. New York: Berkley.

Watson, Charles E. 1991. *Managing With Integrity: Insights From America's CEOs*. New York: Praeger.

Wilder, Anne. 1994. "How to Hold Public Office for 14 Years." *The Tribune*, July 27, pp. A5, A7. Ft. Pierce, FL.

Woodward, Harry and Steve Buchholz. 1987. *After-shock: Helping People Through Corporate Change*. New York: John Wiley & Sons.

INDEX